# The Trials & Tribulations of Nelson the Cat

(Blessed is the cat that remains steadfast under trial)

Written under duress by his Owner
(Erroneous human perspective)

or

*His* Loyal Human Companion
(Correct Feline Perspective)

# Rick Vaughan

**Glossary / Glossaire:**

LHC: Loyal Human Companion

FCH: Fidèle Compagnon Humain

Moggies: Uncouth ruffians, peasants or felines of dubious bloodlines

## Copyright © Rick Vaughan 2013

Rick Vaughan asserts his moral right under the Copyright, Designs and Patents Act, 1988, to be identified as the author of this work. All rights reserved.

Disclaimer: This book is full of news, gossip and rumour. You are invited to use your discretion when discerning which is which. All opinions contained within are that of Nelson, his entourage and his biographer and are not intended to be taken as fact. All rights reserved, including the right to reproduce this book, or portions thereof, in any form. No part of this text may be reproduced, transmitted, downloaded, decompiled, reverse engineered, or stored in or introduced into any information storage and retrieval system, in any form and by any means, whether electronic or mechanical without the express written permission of the publisher and author.

The scanning, uploading, and distribution of this book via the Internet or via any other means without the permission of the publisher is illegal and punishable by law.

Please purchase only authorised electronic/print editions, and do not participate in or encourage electronic/print piracy of copyrighted materials. This book is presented solely for entertainment purposes. No account of any persons living or dead that may be seen to be defamatory are intended as fact – just the opinion of Nelson the Cat and his erstwhile biographer.

The book is written in good humour and while the best efforts have been used in preparing this book, the author and publisher make no representations or warranties of any kind and assume no liabilities of any kind with respect to the accuracy of the contents. Neither the author nor the publisher shall be held liable or responsible to any person or entity with respect to any loss of respect or incidental or consequential damages caused, or alleged to have been caused, directly or indirectly, by the text contained herein.

Original artwork (Front and Back Covers) by Dasha Luchinskaya.

Additional artwork by Chris Canning.

**This edition published in 2013 by Concise Publishing.**

**Also available as an e-book for Kindle and other i-technology.**

**ISBN-13: 978-1491076491**
**ISBN-10: 1491076496**

# The Debacle

**Towards the end of 2011…**

My diary commences with my LHC taking me - as a special treat - to watch the England Rugby Team's attempt to win the Rugby World Cup in New Zealand in late 2011. He had just survived a divorce and, having managed to avoid being bankrupted in legal fees, wanted to treat us both to a holiday.

Luckily, he managed to keep his house in Leeds and his rundown little holiday retreat in rural France. His snooty ex-wife said she regretted agreeing to buy it as she was used to staying in 5-star hotels in the Greek Islands and did not want to spend the first two days in France mowing an overgrown lawn, followed by another day doing the laundry and cooking… she just wanted to relax and read a book, with a glass of Chardonnay in her hand. She added that she envisaged herself beside an obligatory swimming pool, on a sunny day (with a guaranteed minimum temperature of 40 degrees).

So I helpfully suggested she try Chernobyl.

This may explain why my LHC *'gained custody of the cat'* to his ostensibly unbridled joy (though I was not convinced) whilst she got custody of a garden gnome - even though its nose had dropped off.

Her cooking skills were so dire that I once enquired whether she only ever used the Lucrezia

Borgia Recipe Book – after which I got booted out of the house.

On one occasion in France I offered to fill up the bath with cask wine so she could soak in it for hours whilst I read her the first three chapters of 'Cooking for Dummies'… and I was again thrown out of the house!

My LHC intimated on the flight over that he had a little surprise for me…

'Not a one way trip to the Vets for the sacrifice of my reproductive organs?' I enquired anxiously, before sprinting into the Captain's cabin and asking him to turn back immediately - even though we were now over Singapore. I would have hijacked the plane had the cutlery been metal not plastic and had I been tall enough to see out of the front windscreen. This feline mutilation *in extremis* was something his ex-wife had been advocating ever since the day I walked into their house.

'It's only a little operation, he won't feel a thing…' she used to tell him as I instantly crossed my hind legs and my copper eyes widened with unadulterated terror. At times like these my cat flap always seemed to shrink in size.

'…and he'll be much happier for it.'

Of course, I shall be absolutely over the moon - save the bits left in the Vet's Torture Chamber… perhaps someone would like to consult me on this matter before booking any appointments?

'And they can even do it with a rubber band so it doesn't cost much at all.'

Charming. Castrated by the lowest bidding, least skilled torturer of the Spanish Inquisition: simultaneously mutilated and humiliated.

And all this from someone who was always (quite rightly) decrying the practise of female circumcision in Africa (I dread to think what they do to male cats in Africa) but she was perfectly comfortable with the barbaric practise of feline castration in the UK. Always did smack of double standards to me.

I think this helped me to bond with my LHC. He seemed almost as uncomfortable about her argument as I did.

'First the cat, then me...' his alarmed expression said, as he weighed up the pros and cons of this failsafe form of contraception.

And the 21st Century *Lorena Bobbit* wondered why I never liked her and always took inordinate pleasure in sharpening my claws on her 12 pairs of Ugg Boots. She was always complaining too that I kept spraying everywhere - but it was my territory hence I felt it was well within my rights to mark it every now and then just to keep away any low-life moggies.

The divorce had dragged on for two years and, now it was all over, he was hoping that he would meet someone nice - with whom he had something in common, or someone who was at least only borderline psychotic and would like to do more at weekends than just shopping on the High Street.

With the hindsight that can elude my species, I wish I had chosen to decline his offer of a 'once in a lifetime' trip to the Antipodes. As, only when I arrived in Auckland, did I realise that I was to be the England Team's unofficial mascot.

I had intended to update my journal every day in Queenstown (perhaps that location was chosen in honour of our own royal WAG?) but was continually distracted by the outrageous exploits of certain buffoons within the England Rugby Team.

It was made crystal clear to all of us that we were Ambassadors for England and should treat our hosts with the utmost courtesy and respect. No doubt, Richard the Lionheart would have said something similar, and something *equally futile*, to his army of Crusaders before setting off to the Holy Land in 1189.

I am not a particularly diligent student of history as I could not bear to read beyond Merry England during the Middle Ages. I know all about the persecution of my ancestors and their devoted old lady owners who were all burned to death by the superstitious and uneducated imbeciles who thought them incarnations of the devil.

I am Roman Catholic, for God's sake...

I do not know whether the Crusaders in 1189 wore chainmail board shorts and bovver boots, chanting *'Ingerlund, Ingerlund, Ingerlund'* whilst drunkenly rampaging through the previously peaceful beaches and tea houses in Palestine but perhaps the sport of dwarf-throwing started with the captured Saracens, after all, there is an English club side named after Saladin's troops. On the subject of my study of history... I did enjoy Ancient History especially as the Egyptians (quite rightly) revered my ancestors. It is rumoured that the legions of Julius Caesar not only introduced central heating, the ballista, unpronounceable place names, mosaic tiles, socks & sandals (not their best innovation, I have to say) to Ancient Briton, but also introduced felines. This may explain our regal demeanour.

The majestic Monica Bellucci recently played the role of Cleopatra in an enjoyable French historical drama entitled: 'Asterix and Obelix: Mission Cleopatra'.

I assumed that Asterix and his clinicallix obeserix friend Obelix were Gallic heroes on a par with Roland and Oliver but more marketable in the 21st Century - for some reason.

It was rumoured that Caractacus would not go anywhere without his devoted British Blue companion, Mouserix, even when he was sent in chains to Rome - betrayed to the Romans by the Queen of the Brigante. He ended up being a Senator and fêted by Rome, whilst she went off binge-drinking with her hordes of harpies every weekend in Danum…

Going back to the '…have a couple of relaxing beers after the abject performance against the Pumas' (must admit, I was very nervous about meeting them) in Royal WAG Town NZ, I am pleased to say that I behaved impeccably… unlike many of my human companions. I was actually extremely unhappy with them.

Being a well-mannered, sophisticated and debonair chap myself, I would have expected a little more decorum from the Rugby-playing fraternity who decided to partake in an evening of dwarf-throwing. For example, why couldn't they just buy the dwarves a couple of drinks and enjoy a relaxed evening discussing whether England could beat the mighty All Blacks or practise some Morris Dancing as our response to their bizarre, pre-match ritual?

I suppose I should just be grateful they did not turn their inebriated attentions to me viz. Nelson the Cat being Royal WAG Town's equivalent of a lion allegedly fighting off 40 Cambodian Fighting Midgets.

At least the admirably über-professional, points scoring machine, Johnny Wilkicksome did not let England down, on or off the pitch, but his previously impeccable kicking did not quite work the wonders that it had in 2003. Perhaps all of the injuries over the years had finally caught up with him and having watched my first game, I was amazed that anyone could walk off the pitch unaided. Hopefully this outstanding servant to English Rugby may one day become the Head Coach of England and produce a team of champions on the pitch and gentlemen off it. Though if it were me I would not want to give up the Mediterranean lifestyle in France which I imagine would be slightly more agreeable than life on the Tyneside Riviera.

On the other hand, had France adopted Gentleman Johnny and played him at fly-half, I am certain they would have easily won the World Cup.

The picture above is of me sitting incognito in the infamous dwarf-throwing pub in Queenstown.

Certainly this would not have been my choice; being a lover of cool jazz such as Courtney Pine, Denys Baptiste and Soweto Kinch.

However, I tried in vain to find a nice jazz café-bar where I could just relax with a saucer of Jersey Cream and listen to Planet Jazz. Mr Kinch is definitely a cool cat.

I did find it utterly ridiculous that, as a 3-year old feline weighing 6 kilos, I was supposed to keep an eye on a drunken rabble of inebriated 120-kilo humans aged around 30: some of whom proved themselves to be blessed with zero powers of self-awareness or circumspection, bearing in mind that a photo taken on a mobile phone can be instantly sent around the world.

The senior member of the party, Mr Teetotal, was supposed to be setting an example to the younger members of the squad.

I felt compelled to advise him not to get involved in any dwarf throwing or wrestling, but just as I got to the bar and was about to pass him the advice, I was spear tackled by two catapulted midgets. I felt as if I had run into miniature versions of the fearsome Samoan wingers Tu'u Taane Brix and Kurt Moltenlava.

By the time I finally staggered back onto my paws he had disappeared along with his entourage.

Now... if that had been a Premiership Footballer I would not have batted an eyelid. Meanwhile, I was carried off to a local Veterinary Surgery where Doctor O'Driscoll treated me for concussion and a dislocated shoulder.

As I feared, news of the evening's drunken revelry soon spread across the globe and Mrs Teetotal arrived so quickly from her equestrian event in England - presumably to give them all a right royal thrashing with her riding crop - that I can only assume she travelled on Pegasus.

I was mesmerised by the strange ritual being performed by the home team before every game and wondered why they could not have mixed it up occasionally with some Irish dancing.

A friendly Aucklander called Rudy Shepherd told me that this was a traditional welcome for honoured guests, but I would not want to stay for dinner if that was their idea of a friendly salutation.

However, after the fourth viewing of this peculiar ritual, it dawned on me what the real issue was and I started to empathise with and admire them.

I deduced they must have all been suffering from severe constipation and I now recognised their mannerisms and pained facial expressions as being very similar to my own, even as far as extruding their tongues. I extrude my tongue when I have a particularly bad case of constipation which is generally brought on by too much dry cat food – my LHC tells me that is great value as it is ¼ the price of *Cat Master Chef* Coq au Vin and is, in his erudite opinion, just as good.

I beg to differ as I have yet to witness him actually trying to eat the dried, constipation-inducing rubbish. I would prefer to stick to actual Coq au Vin.

It is at times like these that I have to weigh up the pros and cons of cat guerrilla tactics such as climbing up his new velvet curtains. I bet they cost a lot more than a dozen cans of gourmet cat food - which makes me realise where his priorities lie thus I question my own loyalty to him.

I was very impressed that the home team could play 80 minutes of rugby when suffering such huge discomfort. In times of similar distress, I have just enough energy to lie down on my beanbag.

By the time of the final, I was concerned that after the seventh round of this painful ritual they may suddenly be relieved of their afflictions and so I recommended to one of their Coaching Staff that 15 litter trays be placed behind them immediately after the national anthems had been played. It's not much fun being caught out unawares - especially when on global television. His gracious reply to my helpful suggestion was *'Why don't yer \*\*\*\* off back home to Pommieland yer stupid \*\*\*\*\*\*\* mongrel cat'* which I believe may not have been a traditional welcome.

I am called a British Blue because of my unquestionably blue fur. Hence, I realised in one of my more existentialist moments, that I am blue… so I act blue.

But why are they called the All Blacks? Most of them are whiter than my cousins in Scotland.

Which brings me on to some of the names in the squads.

If McAllister is a traditional Japanese surname then call me a sabre-toothed tiger...

But England have Tuilagi (I am not sure if that is a traditional Yorkshire surname) who presumably decided to train for a triathlon by diving into Auckland harbour.

The more cynical Red Rose Supporters could say it was a shame that some of the other members of the squad did not follow suit and jump with him...

Going back to the off-colour, All Blacks' (no doubt due to their affliction) pre-match ritual, I was very disappointed that the French XV did not respond with the can-can. Plus, it was a shame that the two metre giant Jean-Luc Chasseur des Laineux-Mammouths was omitted from the French XV.

Beatrice, my current French belle, is a lovely Chartreuse who resides in a rundown little chateau near Chauvigny and loves playing traditional Parisian café-bar music on the accordion. She believes that, in reply to the All Blacks' pre-match ritual, he could have led the French squad in a formidable rendition of the Can-Can which would have given Les Bleus the edge in the Final which they so nearly won.

If only President Sarkozy had granted French Citizenship to Gentilhomme Jean...

The highlight of the entire tournament for me was listening to the marvellous Italian national anthem which is even nicer than 'La Marseillaise'. I noticed the Italians standing speechless and becoming very emotional (perhaps they were embarrassed as they did not know the words apart from Italia: they obviously had no naturalised Pacific Islanders in their squad) and it took them twenty minutes to regain their composure, by which point the opposing teams had clocked up 15 points.

I failed to mention that whilst I was having to associate myself with this under-performing, ambassadorial rabble, my LHC was treating himself to a luxury outbound holiday in the South Island - consisting of wild pig shooting, sky diving and MTB which I believe is an acronym for Mountain Biking - whilst I had to settle for Mister Teetotal Blottoed.

## January

**La drôlerie des rosbifs**

I resigned in disgust from my position as unofficial Team Mascot of the lamentable England Rugby Team.

One of my ancestors was Chief Mouser on HMS Victory, where he was occasionally treated to fresh cream and rum in the Admiral's Cabin, so I have certain high principles, which that ill-disciplined team of misfits failed to meet. Some of them should have been locked up in the Tower... or Murrayfield, at least.

We duly arrived back home with, upon arrival, my LHC referring to everyone as 'dude' but it wasn't long before the drudgery of working 50 hours a week and returning home in the dark, plus being a slave to unreasonable deadlines, had taken their toll on his adventurous spirit and he lamented at not having met '…a nice Polynesian lass' in the land of the long, white cloud'.

I did think it strange and optimistic *in extremis* to hope to meet a Polynesian in Wales.

Must be Post-Holiday Depression, dude… plus his £7,500 credit card bill, I mused, as sympathetically as possible, bearing in mind the time that I had endured in the land of the long, white, underperforming, England rugby shirt.

On the other hand, I was delighted to be back! Admittedly, I did not have to go out to work for 50 hours each week. But the football season was in full swing with Celtic looking to be on track to yet another title and qualification for the Champions League. And… I had holidays in France to look forward to, where I could meet up again with the delectable Beatrice.

Nearing the end of the month, we went down to *The Merry Monk* for a quiet drink of beer… and milk - even though it was quiz night with the locals - who I assumed must be in-bred, as they were so stupid.

Quizmaster:
What is the name of the Russian Bird that migrates from the Arctic Tundra to China each winter?

The Team next to us pompously called themselves 'The Scholarly Scholars'. All eight of them were schoolteachers… and they wonder why the State School system is going to the dogs…

Total silence – two minutes earlier they had told myself, my LHC and his drinking mate to be quiet -

as they could not concentrate on their quiz with all of the people rudely talking in a pub… sans ironie.

They asked for another two minutes as this was a toughie and they had been distracted presumably by myself and my fellow bell-ringing Monks.

The Quizmaster gave them 15 seconds so they then complained about me *supposedly* making a loud slurping noise when I was drinking my second saucer of milk and demanded another thirty seconds otherwise…

'…we're not playing any more and we'll insist on having our £1 entry fee back'.

'Arrogant prigs… they must be Secondary School teachers.' I purred, just loud enough for one particularly mournful looking teacher to hear. He wore big, black, retro National Health Service glasses which accentuated his doleful demeanour.'

'What did you call me?' asked Professor Smith miserably, as he stared accusingly at my LHC - whose idea of having a relaxing evening over a couple of beers was beginning to unravel.

Before he could apologise to Professor Smith I continued…

'I am terribly sorry sir. I did not realise the cuts to the Education Budget had hit teachers so hard. Which just goes to show; you learn something new every day.'

I was now starting to enjoy the evening, having been bored witless for the past ninety minutes, listening to my LHC drone on to his drinking partner Kevin the Cocksure Cost Accountant about the fact he could not find a new mate.

'You want to take a leaf out of my book matey and enrol on an Internet dating website. Only costs me £65 a month. I've been out with 23 women already, only 15 of whom were married. As soon as I tell them I'm a Cost Accountant I have them banging my door down. I did embellish my profile a bit saying I was 5' 9" rather than 5'4".'

Turning to his scholarly accuser, my pusillanimous human companion tried to make the situation less combustible by apologising 'for his rude cat'.

'If your cat is so clever, perhaps he would like to tell us what the answer is? We have 13 Degrees and 4 HNCs between us and we just don't know the answer.'

'A sputnik sparrow,' I immediately replied with the self-assured panache of Flashman himself.

'A sputnik bloody sparrow???

Do you seriously expect me to…'

'Yeah, that's it chuck. I was juss gonna say Spootneek Sparra. I deserve another Smirnoff Ice fir gittin that right,' …burst out a clearly worse for wear Head of Biology from the Wirral.

They duly handed in their answer sheet which led to some guffawing on the part of the Quizmaster.

'Is it really a Sputnik Sparrow?' asked my disappointingly gullible honorary member of the RSPB.

'I reckon it's a White-Tailed Russian Buzzard. It's the one you see on all their military cap badges. I've got one on my Ushanka here, ' said cocksure Kevin who was even less deserving of honorary membership of the RSPB. Then, to prove his point, he proudly put on his Ushanka - clearly feeling like a million roubles.

'But that's double-headed. I've never seen a double-headed eagle before,' queried my ornithologically challenged LHC …

'The correct answer is actually the Siberian White Crane,' I said with the faintest of Cheshire Cat-like grins, which cocky Kev, with an Auditor's unerring ability to sense something afoot, had picked up on.

'I've never met a cat that could talk before. Well then, my clever, little, furry, feline friend, I've got a joke for you. What do you call a French cat's favourite dessert?!'

'Are you referring to a Chartreux, par écheance?'

'A what ? Isn't that some type of liqueur made by Trappist Monks in Belgium?'

'I've had an idea Kev. Let's go back to you boasting about your success on Internet dating.'

'The liqueur that you incorrectly named is actually called Chartreuse which was first made in 1764 by the Carthusian monks in Fr....'
'All right, can you please just answer my question??'

'Could it, by any chance, be mousse au chocolat?'

After a pause, he turned away indignantly and resumed giving his dating advice to my forlorn LHC.

'I've been telling you for ages: just give it a go. What have you got to lose? They're not all psychos or alcoholics on there and you can't meet your ex-wife as she is in Australia.'

'Maybe I should give it a go as I've had less luck than my cat who got himself fixed up with a French artist's cat in Montmorillon.'

'What's her owner like? French... must be exotic. Why not check her out?

'She's a lesbian.'

'That wouldn't put me off. She might have a nice girlfriend. More the merrier. You could fly over every weekend and, what's that French expression, enjoy a *ménage à trois*.'

At this point I feared the conversation was going to descend into the gutter, so I enquired as to whether my saucer of milk could be topped up. This invited the scorn of the accounting lothario.

'So then, Romeo the Cat, what's the name of your feline French floozy then: Cattyrine Deneuve or Kitty Bardot?'

'Her name is Beatrice. Fancy another Deuchars?' responded my LHC, hoping to change the subject, but the accountant was in full flight.

I sat there impassively thinking that he's more stupid than the Scholarly Scholars.

'In a minute. I've got a couple of jokes about girls called Beatrix, which I must tell your cat.'

'An accounting comedian… now there's an oxymoron if ever there was one. Whatever next, a carnivorous vegetarian?'

'An oxy what? Anyway Top Cat, what do you call a girl who can balance a pint of Guinness on one shoulder, a pint of Landlord on the other, and a pint of Heineken on her head?'

Knowing what he was going to say next I ignored him and just looked at my LHC to express my annoyance that:

a. My saucer was empty.
   b. I was the butt of this buffoon's jokes.

'Beatrix!! Get it?? Ha ha...'

He could barely contain himself to the point that I was hoping he might do us all a favour and internally combust. My LHC tried in vain to spike his mortars of mirth.

'Did you say that yours was a pint of Timmy Taylor, Kev? How about you come with me to the bar as they've got about seven real ales on this evening and the bar closes in ten minutes?'

'How about a quart of Hemlock Best Bitter for our bean counting jester?' I suggested but, whilst my LHC just shook his head, the mirth-ridden jester did not hear me.

'Got another joke before I come with you to the bar. What do you call a girl who can balance a pint of Ruddles on one shoulder, a pint of John Smith's on the other, and a pint of Carlsberg... this is brilliant, you'll love this one... on her head - whilst beating everyone in the pub at pool?'

A moment of silence ensued as I refused to take the bait.

'Beatrix Potter!!!!'

'Boom boom. I can see why you have so many women dropping down at your feet with that rapier-like wit of yours.' I dryly replied.

At this point, my LHC brusquely picked me up and carried me to the bar; as though I was the one at fault.

'Now look, I know he can be a bit overbearing and full of himself, but his heart is in the right place and he is trying to cheer me up with some helpful advice. So just be nice to him and please don't answer him back, okay?'

'Get that bloody cat off the bar. He's a health hazard. We'll all go down with E.coli which won't look good as we've just taken on a new Chef from Bangkok and had our first curry night,' rudely interrupted a spotty-faced member of the bar staff who looked like he was paid in beer tokens and cigarettes, rather than cash, and had never been washed *or deloused* in his life before.

'Judging by the state of yourself, my dear barman, I would hazard to guess you may be immune to even the most virulent biological strains that the world has to offer.' I couldn't resist responding, just in case he wanted to make any Beatrix Potter-themed jokes too.

'One more comment like that and the cat's barred. If it were up to me, I wouldn't let either cats or dogs in. We got 5 stars for our hygiene standards last month and we've had no cases of salmonella here…

since we changed our poultry supplier last October.' He said, before sneezing all over a pile of fresh tea-towels.

'Before you get us both kicked out, let's get back to Kev. I reckon it might be worth a go this Internet dating lark. He's obviously been successful and he's not exactly an oil painting. So just be nice, as I need some tips from him. And just remember how kind-hearted and supportive he was to me when I was going through my divorce.'

'Are you referring to his offer of a £20,000 loan over 4 years with an APR of 999%?'

'It was actually 9.99%. Plus a free pint of *Tripel Karmeliet* every week for the first two years.'

We sat down and immediately my tormentor continued…
'I see… Felix - that you're on your fourth saucer of milk tonight. Are you trying to set a new lap record?… Why can't a cat commit suicide?'

Silent paws.

'Because it's got nine lives! Now… you don't look like you're enjoying my jokes. Or is it because your milk has gone off which I suppose would make you a Sourpuss? Boom boom! Ha ha…'

'Where is Basil Brush when you need him?' I thought, deciding I preferred listening to him boast about all the women he supposedly had drooling over him.

'On the contrary, this evening has been most enjoyable, especially as I have never before met anyone from the accounting profession who possessed such a fine sense of humour.'

'Nice to see a cat that can laugh at itself. I had always thought cats were haughty, dull and humourless and had inflated opinions of themselves.'

'Would these be Cat Accountants, by any chance?'

Judging by the blank look on his face the answer to that was possibly not.

'As you two are both Catholics, you'll like this one. What does a religious cat read every Sunday?'

A dignified silence ensued.

'Go on, have a go…!'

I thought '…if he gets any more excited I'll have to go home and fetch my litter tray'. And… as if he was one of Pavlov's' less cerebral canines, my LHC felt compelled to answer: 'The Book of Felines?'

'No!' replied the Master of Ceremonies.
'Come on Top Cat, have a guess!'

'Cycling Plus?'

'Of course not. Don't be so ridiculous. It is of course… a **'cat**echism**'**.

'Well, knock me down with a punchline…' I thought, wearily. 'I would never have guessed that one.'

Just got one more joke, which is appropriate for a Francophile cat, such as yourself. What is a cat's favourite food when it's on holiday in France? Come on, you should know the answer to this.'

'If it was me I would choose, assuming of course that I had the acquiescence of my faithful human companion: une assiette de viandes froides for the Hors d'Oeuvre followed by canard à l'orange with haricots verts and pommes de terre dauphinoise for an Entrée and finished off - not with a witty dollop of mousse au chocolat - but with crêpes suzette. I would, however, wager that the answer you were looking for may have been *ratatouille*?'

A longer silent paws ensued, which was interrupted by the hygiene award-winning, E.coli carrying barman calling *time*.

'But I must say that my life has been enriched by your witty asides, so please may I reciprocate with a joke of my own…' (A rhetorical question, hence no question mark, in case the Scholarly Scholars are reading this).

'What do you call someone who marries the most beautiful actress in the world for her money…?

'No idea.'

Silence ensued for what seemed an eternity.

'An Accountant.'

'An Accountant???' they both asked in unison.

The ensuing silence was broken by Anthrax Andy (The Barman) asking everyone to drink up before sneezing violently over a freshly poured pint of Plague Black Ale.

'Oh, I get it now. I like that one. That's actually quite good Nelson. I'll use that in my Xmas Epistle this year, so hopefully I won't be accused of being dull and boring ever again.'

'And I've just got one more, before we have to take our leave. What do you call someone who marries the most beautiful actress in the world for her money then won't let her spend any of it…?'

No reply.

'…A Cost Accountant. **Boom boom,**' at which point I took a step backwards… out of kicking distance.

Kevin retreated back to his world of Internet dating successes, as though he was an online dating version of Baron von Richthofen regaling newly-arrived pilots with his exploits.

As we departed – with me in the doghouse with a quiz team, two non-participants and Anthrax Andy, my LHC promised Kevin the ledger-keeping Lothario that he would finally give Internet dating a one-off go next month - though he remained unconvinced.

When we got back, I did offer to help him write up a witty profile, but he declined on account of… 'trusting me about as far as he could throw me' - which he said, '…would ideally be over the garden wall, out of Leeds, past Hull and thence into the North Sea.'

If he threw me that far then he could give Jessica Ennis a run for her money in the javelin section of the Heptathlon.

# February

**Sad tidings from Montmorillon**

No snow so far this winter: perhaps global warming has finally started and I can look forward to a long, hot, dry, rodent-chasing summer this year.

I received some very sad news from France. Beatrice's FCH has taken her to Haiti to live on a communal farm that produces organic coffee for the bohemian bars in the 5th Arrondissement of Paris. I said that I would happily pop over via Eurotunnel until she pointed out that it is an island somewhere in the Caribbean.

I have a silver tabby cousin in Barbados called Winston (he's also a British Shorthair but born in Barbados). This country cannot be far away from Haiti, so I could visit both of them, if I could persuade my LHC to pay for my airfare.

Now that he has bought a holiday home in a quaint little hamlet just a vole's throw away from Montmorillon, asking him for any financial help might be difficult, as, for the last few years, he has spent all of his holidays at his French retreat. He wants to get his money's worth out of the house.

Montmorillon is not an obvious tourist attraction, being nothing like Ibiza or any of the Greek Islands. Dieu merci. This means that he does not have to mix with the low-life class of British Tourists who wear Union Jack shorts, make no effort to speak the local language but resort to shouting instead, get drunk every night, moan about the beer and food and try to slip away from bars without paying.

Having had a few early morning runs around the Cité de l'écrit (it is the smallest city I've ever seen) then back to the little hamlet where we have our 'maison de vacances' or 'Rix Château' as Louis XIV calls it, it is indeed a very sleepy but pleasant little place. Its residents must be very devout Catholics, as Montmorillon has two huge churches so, I suppose, if they feel one Priest is overly-pontificating during his sermon they can simply pop over to the other church.

It has been designated as the City of Writers but, as far as I am aware, Victor Hugo was not Montmorillonaise. I really like passing the artists' studios and a great little pottery shop, though I don't know how the potter makes any money as her shop is always closed - even when the sign on her door states uncategorically 'Ouvert'.

The River Gartempe flows through the town, and it is great for catching trout and salmon, though it is a bit too deep and fast-flowing for me. Despite signs stating 'Interdit la pêche au saumon' the local French seem to fish for anything with a healthy disregard for authority.

King Louis's favourite bar is 'Le paradis des Trappistes' which is a delightful bar serving over 200 Belgian beers. He raves on so much about this bar that I am surprised he doesn't move in, but I am tempted to try one of the beers as they seem to have the same effect on the local humans as cat mint has on des chats chartreux. It even has a huge display of the famous French hero Asterix.

In downtown Montmorillon sits the Hôtel de Strasbourg, with its superb restaurant, and next to it is the slightly less salubrious 'Le Marchand' bar which does have a delightful spot overlooking a crossroads by the bridge, where one can while away many an hour guessing when the next car accident will occur.

It also boasts the most popular haunt of all les rosbifs within a 30 kilometre radius… so it could possibly be the liveliest bar in Poitou-Charentes, especially when a band is playing - as the French seem to avoid drinking in bars in the evening. Perhaps they wish to avoid les rosbifs?

Across the bridge is Rick Hinault's favourite shop… in the whole of France: Le Magasin Vélo-Sport, even though, after 5 years of admiring the beautiful bikes in the shop window, le blaireau rosbif has yet to buy anything from it '…*perhaps this is another example of Internet shopping putting independent shopkeepers out of business'*, I thought dolefully, though he seems to spend all of his time either renovating the house or in France's most useless DIY store 'NCSV' (Nos Coffres Sont Vides) looking for items that they never seem to have in stock. But the staff are always very friendly to me, so I quite enjoy our visits whilst he always leaves empty-handed and in a foul mood.

Montmorillon is very quiet, apart from Wednesday mornings when there is a local farmers' market in town, which seems to be the only time Le pont du chêne opens for business.

The City's main claim to fame is that it's the macaroon-making capital of France (their macaroons may be quite delightful but my miserly LHC won't give me one.) It also seems to be the baguette capital of France, as there is a boulangerie on every street.

Unfortunately, since he bought the rundown house, he has become totally obsessed with renovating it and now bores everyone to death with his newly-mastered vocabulary of French plumbing and electrics such as: 'Nelson, have a guess what "une plafonnière" is.'

My tart response was thus:

'If I knew what 'une plafonnière' was then I should be enrolled on an Apprentice Electrician's Course in Poitiers.' I then stunned him with my answer viz. 'a ceiling fan'. Touché.

The buffoon obviously forgot that I had to accompany him on his thrice-daily trip to 'NCSV' for an entire fortnight last summer.

This shop truly is the most useless hardware store I have ever come across: the DIY equivalent of a butcher's shop in Haiti or Havana. There is NEVER anything in it, apart from some over-priced garden furniture, the odd lamp and a sundry selection of cheap dog toys. However, one day it actually contained a (presumably once in a lifetime consignment) of plafonnières (ceiling fans).

I then went on to list the words and phrases that would be of infinitely more use to me. I have attempted to write these essential phrases in French first. Please excuse any errors as French is not my first language and the miser will not pay for me to attend night classes at Leeds Met Uni.

1. Mon repas favori est bœuf bourguignon mais je ne suis pas impartial aux crêpes au jambon.

2. Je ne peux pas manger des cuisses des grenouilles parce qu'elles se bloqueront dans ma gorge.

3. Est-ce que le camembert va bien avec un campagnol ?

4. Est-ce que le fromage de chèvre donne la diarrhée aux chats ?

5. Tu es un chat chartreuse adorable.

6. Est-ce que tu as des puces ?

7. Tu as les yeux de cuivre les plus jolies

8. Tu as été soigné récemment contre les vers ?

9. Tu es très jolie mais je sors seulement avec des chats pedigrees (à l'exception des chats siamois)

10. Tu habite dans un château ?

11. Mon loisir favori est de chasser des canards. C'est à toi aussi ?

12. Étant existentialiste, je refuse de faire appliquer pour un permis de pêche dans la Gartempe.

13. Il y a des champs de l'herbe aux chats près de chez moi ?

14. Quelle est la meilleure méthode pour abattre un faisan adulte ?

15. Pourquoi est-ce que des chiens sont permis de rester dans les hôtels en France ?

16. De tous les chiens dans le monde, ceux-là que je méprise le plus sont beagles.

17. Ce serait possible de devenir membre de la chasse des sangliers ?

18. *(Si la réponse à la question précédente est Oui)* Très bon. La chasse commencera à quelle heure le demain matin ?

19. Si les chasseurs ne peuvent pas traquer et capturer des sangliers est-ce qu'ils pourront tirer sure les beagles au lieu?

20. C'est possible d'acheter la crème fraîche de l'île de Jersey n'importe où dans Poitou-Charentes?

21. Tu connais des vétos qui ressemblent Emmanuelle Béart ?

22. C'est vrai que la nourriture sèche pour chats est interdite en France ?

23. *(Si la réponse à la question précédente est Oui)* Comment je fais une demande en vue d'obtenir la citoyenneté française?

24. Je préfère de saumon frais plutôt que du saumon en boîte.

25. **Si je rencontrais un chat socialiste**: Moi-même, je n'aurais jamais voté non plus pour le Président Sarkozy parce qu'il préfère les chiens aux chats.

26. **Si je rencontrais un chat de droite:** Je suis d'accord avec la politique de Aimée Toutlemonde concernant l'expulsion de tous les beagles nord-africains.

27. **Si je rencontrais un chat anarchiste:** Je nommerais Mathieu Allezengrève en tant que président de la France puis attendrais que le parti de commencer !

28. Pour mon petit déjeuner, je voudrais deux croissants avec du beurre et de confiture de framboises, s'il vous plaît.

29. J'aime aller courir tous les matins à quatre heures trente donc je serais reconnaissant si tu pourrais garantir que mon petit déjeuner serait prêt à cinq heures quinze.

30. De quelle taille sont les serpents qui vivent ici ?

31. Mon bac à litière est plein. Pourriez-vous avoir la gentillesse de le vider.

32. J'enverrais tous les chiens de France à la maison nouvelle de Guillaume Taxe de Séjour en Russie.

33. Je préfère rugby plus que le foot mais j'aime le cyclisme surtout.

34. Est-ce que des chats chartreux souffrent de la rage ?

35. Pour moi le point culminant de mon 'année est à regarder Le Tour de France.

36. C'est vrai qu'un seul frelon peut tuer un chat ou un être humain ?

37. Je voudrais acheter cinq kilos de litière pour chat bio s'il vous plaît.

38. Croyez-vous vraiment que Chris Froome pourrait gagner le Tour de France?

39. Ce serait possible acheter des marchandises utiles du Tour de France comme un collier jaune pour chat ou un jouet de l'herbe aux chats qui ressemble El Diablo?

40. Chiens acceptés. Interdit aux chats. Pourquoi ?

**41. Mon fidèle compagnon humain est un bouffon agréable. Et le tien aussi ?**

The English translations are detailed below:

1. 'My favourite meal is boeuf bourguignon but I am not impartial to ham pancakes.'

2. 'I cannot eat frog's legs as they get stuck in my throat.'

3. 'Does Camembert go with vole?'
4. 'Does Goat's cheese give cats diarrhoea?
5. 'You are a cute Chartreuse.'
6. 'Do you have fleas?'
7. 'You have the nicest copper eyes.'
8. 'Have you been wormed recently?'
9. 'You are very pretty but sadly I only go out with pedigree cats (with the notable exception of Siamese).'
10. 'Do you live in a chateau?'
11. 'My favourite hobby is chasing ducks.'
12. 'Being an existentialist, I refuse to apply for a licence to go fishing in the Gartempe.'
13. 'Are there any catmint fields near my house?'
14. 'What is the most effective way to bring down an adult pheasant?'
15. 'Why are dogs allowed to stay overnight in hotels in France?'
16. 'Of all the dogs in the world, the ones I despise most are Beagles.'
17. 'Is it possible to join the wild boar hunt?'
18. (If Yes) 'Goodo. At what time does the hunt start tomorrow morning?'
19. 'If the hunters cannot track down any wild boar can they shoot the Beagles instead?'
20. 'Is it possible to buy fresh Jersey Cream anywhere in Poitou-Charentes?'
21. 'Do you know any vets who look like Emmanuelle Béart?'
22. 'Is it true that dry cat food is banned in France?'
23. (If Yes) 'How do I apply for French citizenship?'

24. 'I prefer fresh salmon rather than out of a tin.'

25. **(If I were to meet a socialist Chartreuse)** 'I would never have voted for President Sarkozy either, because he prefers dogs to cats.'

26. **(If I were to meet a right-wing Chartreuse)** 'I agree with Aimée Toutlemonde's policy of deporting all North African beagles.'

27. **(If I were to meet an anarchist Chartreuse)** 'I would appoint Mathieu Allezengrève as President, then wait for the party to begin!'

28. 'For breakfast, I would like two croissants with butter and raspberry jam please.'

29. 'I like to go for a run every morning at 4.30 a.m. so I would be obliged if you could ensure that my breakfast is ready at 5.15 a.m.'

30. 'How big are the snakes around here?'

31. 'My litter tray is full. Could you be so kind as to empty it.'

32. 'I would send all the dogs in France to Guillaume Taxe de Séjour's new house in Russia.'

33. 'I prefer rugby to football but most of all I like cycling.'

34. 'Do any Chartreux have rabies?'

35. 'The highlight of my year is watching the Tour de France.'

36. 'Is it true that a single hornet can kill a cat or human?'

37. 'I would like to buy 5 kilos of organic cat litter please.'

38. 'Do you really believe Chris Froome could win Le Tour de France this year?'

39.  'Is it possible to buy useful Tour de France merchandise such as a yellow flea collar or an El Diablo catnip toy?'

40.  'Dogs allowed. Cats forbidden. Why?'

**41.  'My loyal human companion is a likeable buffoon. Is yours too?'**

At this point, for some reason, he didn't want to hear any more. I've never been served dinner so quickly in my life. I have hence decided that 'un bouffon' is a much more useful noun from my perspective than 'une plafonnière'.

Unfortunately, I have had to undergo this linguistic torture for 45 minutes each evening before my dinner.

His favourite boast is that his command of French is now so formidable that he doesn't even know the English translation for words plucked from the depths of French plumbing such as 'un poussoir' (a push button located on top of a toilet which one depresses with one's paw or finger in order to flush away the contents). Quite simple really - unless you are 'un bouffon'…

But I have to give him some credit: these are a quantum leap away from the life-saving phrases that have taken him over 3 years of night classes to master such as:

1.  J'ai un poney des Îles Shetland.

2.  Quand ma perruche est malade elle va chez le véto.

3.  Mon gâteau n'est pas formidable.

4.  Aujourd'hui nous portons des tricots verts (ou moins formellement) on porte des tricots verts.

5. Je voudrais bien grignoter vos macarons.
6. Où est le port le plus proche ?
7. Je voudrais voler au lune.
8. Le bain ne marche pas.
9. Je ne suis pas sapeur-pompier. Je suis homme-grenouille mi-temps.
10. Les crocodiles sont allés à la mairie à quatorze heures trente.

**11. Mon chat n'est pas reconnaissant de quelque chose que je lui fasse.**

12. Enchanté de faire votre connaissance, Madame. Je m'appelle Oui Oui.

The English translations are as follows:
1. 'I have a Shetland Pony.'
2. 'When my budgie is ill, it goes to the Vet's.'
3. 'My cake is not tremendous.'
4. 'Today we are wearing green sweaters.'
5. 'I would really like to nibble your macaroons.'
6. 'Where is the nearest port?'
7. 'I would like to fly to the moon.'
8. 'The bath is not working.'
9. 'I am not a fireman. I am a part-time frogman.'
10. 'The crocodiles went to the Town Hall at 2:30 p.m.'
11. **'MY CAT DOES NOT APPRECIATE ANYTHING I DO FOR IT.'**
12. 'Delighted to meet you, Madam. My name is Noddy.'

Apparently he mastered Number 11 straightaway, which did make me adopt a Rodin-like pose and ponder why - as I had promised not to sharpen my claws on his new handmade Chinese Rug (which was to be his pride & joy when it arrived later in the year). And… I hadn't gone to sleep on his head for at least six weeks.

Anyway, I decided to drop Winston a letter and ask what he thought about my visiting both Barbados and Haiti.

I should have known that having lived with a cannabis-smoking Rastafarian for all of his 5 human years (*making him 35 in reality*) it would take a while to get a reply which, whilst well-intentioned, was not the reply that I was looking for. Winston is the only British Shorthair I know who has dreadlocks and wears a multi-coloured woolly cap and Oakley M Frames all the time: he claims a Tasmanian Fast Bowler gave them to him during a test match between the West Indies and Australia, though, I suspect, he purloined them during the luncheon interval of the second day.

He is, however, a fine cricketer and was always in demand until he was banned for 2 seasons for not giving the ball back when fielding in the slips against a team from St Vincent and the Grenadines. This was extended by another three seasons for placing 2 kilos of cannabis in the team's tea urn.

According to Winston, the opinion of the Team Captain was that it was the finest tea he had ever imbibed in his 25 years in the game, even better than the delectably fragrant *Darlinks English Breakfast* - which was twice as expensive.

Unfortunately, Winston's unorthodox sugar-substitute took effect 45 minutes later just as the Captain opened the batting for the Barbadian Buccaneers. The game had to be abandoned 18 minutes later when the by now highly-drugged up, hallucinating and truly buccaneering skipper chased after everyone in the stands and clobbered all and sundry with his bat (having decided they were all giant rats and a blight on humanity.) After spending 9 months in jail for the assault & battery of 16 members of the Bridgetown Rotary Club, he has since been treated for mild schizophrenia for which Winston had to foot the bill out of his own rum and cream allowances.

As with all British Shorthairs, Winston is a relaxed, easy-going and even-tempered cat - who shares my love of Jazz and was over the moon (which is admittedly quite a regular occurrence due to his over-indulgence in ganja) when I sent him a Soweto Kinch CD for Christmas.

He purrs with a delightful Bajan patois which always charms the collars off any lady cats but he also writes in this same patois, making it very difficult for me to understand what on earth he is going on about. I could try calling him on his mobile phone, but the signal is always very weak, due to all the hurricanes.

My point in case is his reply as follows:

'Yo mon, Am kool. Y'all kool too? Ah doan lak dee ideahh aff y'all goan taa Aiitee. Dee ole plaiz got dee Aids. Humains ann dee kats tuu weetch azz tuutaallee boogurd uup dee tuureezum.

Opp u iz well cuz, Wee gatt dee bluudee urrekanz cumin agin tuuneet. Betta guu ann batten doon dee attchazz onn mee uuzz.

Stoopeed wedamon seez eet guuna bee beet weendy tuuneet. Muz tink eezza bluudee komeedeeann. Ah ope ee gettz nuuterd. Tankzz fur dee Jazz Plannatt Cee Dee. Well kool mon.

Owzit guinn wid dee Fraanch guurlfrenn?'

Whilst I appreciated getting details of that evening's weather report from Winston, I assumed he must have eaten too much cannabis with his cat food, bearing in mind the paramount reason for my correspondence was how I could get to see my French girlfriend now that she had emigrated to Haiti.

My curt reply was: No, it was not going particularly well with the French girlfriend as she was now living thousands of miles away with a bunch of hippy eco-friendly humans in a farm called 'La coopérative de café d'arc-en-ciel' , just outside Port-au-Prince.

To which my feline Lothario of a cousin jocularly asked (after getting me to translate the name 'The Rainbow Coffee Co-operative' which, on first impressions, he thought might be a new type of skunk available in the suburbs of Bridgetown… whether she was good looking. If so he would pop over to Port-au-Prince to say 'Yo, mon' and take his chances.

I had a chuckle at that; the cheeky, spliffed-out, young rascal.

A week later I get an email from Beatrice!

Hurrah!! That has made my day.

My spirits soar and I leap around, as though I had a freshly caught, half-dead mouse to play with.

Is ma chèrie coming back to France?

Or better still, will *mon amour* relocate to England so we can be together?

Perhaps we can get married and even have kittens of our own one day?

She told me that she had spent all day, every day, sitting on the beach looking towards the British Isles pining for me. By this point, my heart was pounding.

She had even contemplated jumping aboard a UN Peacekeeping Force airplane, which, despite being owned by the Royal Norwegian Air Force, would have at least got her back to Bergen. The stress had caused her to lose weight and her fur had started to fall out.

Reading this, my eyes were welling up and I felt compelled to book a flight and rescue my darling damsel in distress.

Then she said that two days ago, out of the blue, she had met a wonderful, charming, dreadlocked silver tabby (who otherwise looked like me). He told her that he had swum all the way from Barbados to meet her. She felt it must have been *Kismet* as it was love at first sight and that they were getting married next week.

Kismet??? It felt more like perfidy to me. I had been betrayed by my own Judas.

To add several barrel loads of salt (or dry cat food) to my wounds, she then felt compelled to patronise my tortured and bewildered soul with platitudes reserved solely for cuckolds.

Hope you are well. Gotta go, as we are late for a beach BBQ.

(Thank you for rubbing my nose in it by reminding me that it is -15 degrees Celsius here, there is a raging blizzard outside so I cannot open my cat flap and my LHC is too tight-fisted to put the central heating on until 9.00 p.m. when *HE* gets home.)

It was great whilst it lasted but all good things come to an end.

(Yep, hopefully an unneutered cousin…)

I'll send you back your ping pong balls if you wish?

(Thank you, but I rather fancy said cousin will find a more pressing use for them after he has been neutered.)

Time is a great healer.

(Not when neutering is involved.)

It's not you, it's me.

(Thank you for stating the blindingly obvious.)

I still really like you.

(Thank you for stating the not-so blindingly obvious.)

I hope we can still be friends.

(Of course. Please send me an invitation to the wedding, as I would love to be Best Cat.)

Take care. Wish you all the best, Beatrice xxx

(Farewell Delilah. By the way, cannabis abuse eventually leads to schizophrenia.)

P.S. By the way, I really like your 'Planet Jazz' CD so would you mind if we play that instead of the traditional *'Here Comes The Bride'* when I make my entrance into the cathedral?

Of course, why not? And for good measure why don't you plunge a dagger through my heart, time and again, until you have taken away all my nine lives, you heartless strumpet ?

You may have deduced that my emotions had got the better of my laid-back and mild-mannered personality by this point.
That night, I made two voodoo dolls out of a couple of old cat nip toys - paying particular attention to the one with dreadlocks - and prayed that the Tonton Macoute of Creole mythology (or the Tontons Macoutes of real-life Haiti) would capture them and make them suffer.
Admittedly this is not the kind of prayer that God really wants to hear.

# March

**Bohemians in Paris**

Nipped over to Paris where it exceeded 25 degrees. Summer has come early. Hurrah! After three consecutive days of sunshine in England the water authorities up and down the country sprang into action and imposed hosepipe bans with immediate effect.

My loyal human companion sneaked me in to Le Stade de France to watch Stade Français get pipped 21-18 by Toulouse.

I quite fancy myself as their team mascot dressed *en rose*. They even had pink goalposts.

Elegance and class: a winning combination though, sadly, not on this occasion.

For some reason they had a fireworks display after the game (perhaps they had magnanimously moved La Fête Nationale from 14th July just for us) which scared the living daylights out of me. Either that or it was the booming, accompanying music by AC/DC (I would rather have chosen to listen to Debussy or la délicieuse Patricia Kaas). Perhaps Angus Young lives in France (in which case, he should replace his school cap with a French or Basque beret).

My LHC was over the moon when over the tannoy system came his favourite *AC/DC* song, which sounded to me like a *'Whole lot of Rosbifs'*, and which they presumably played especially for us; being the only rosbifs in the 72,000 crowd of Frenchmen. I thought that was a very nice touch and much more upbeat than *'God Save the Queen.'*

As a special treat that evening my LHC gave me a lamb kebab, couscous and a bowl of goat's milk in the Paris Mosque where I made an acquaintance with a beautiful Chartreuse whose FCH was an art dealer who resided in a 5$^{th}$ floor apartment in Montparnasse and rode an MP3 Piaggio Scooter. We exchanged ear tagging chip numbers in the hope that I may see her again. To quote my namesake and hero, it was *Kismet* rather than perchance.

Being a quixotic gent, I offered her a morsel of my kebab, which made her purr serenely (it was as if I had met Debussy's cat… I was in cat heaven) which, in turn, made my whiskers jump up and down like a can-can dancer's legs. Then I went weak at the knees and was eternally grateful to *mon Dieu* that I had not been neutered. I also gallantly offered to run down to the local Place Monge Métro Station and catch a live black rat, but she declined this as she is used to her FCH feeding her only Coquilles Saint Jacques and Boeuf Limousine.

This did make me wonder if I was out of my arrondissement as I am lucky if my LHC even deigns to give me the remains of his fish 'n' chips - and this is the really claw-curlingly, cringingly embarrassing part – they are usually wrapped in *The Daily Drivel.* Why could he not display a soupçon of sophistication for once and eat them out of Le Monde or Le Figaro? I'd even settle for them being wrapped in L'Équipe…

Another faux pas (énorme) on my part occurred when she excitedly told me all about her favourite

French authors whom she had studied for her BA (Hons) in French Literature at La Sorbonne. This went on for almost 2 hours. She purred that her favourite novel of all time was Thérèse Raquin then… the moment I was dreading. She asked me for **my** views on Thérèse Raquin, '…which she anticipated with alacrity'.

With who…?

I looked round the dimly-lit, smoky café-bar and could see no-one else within earshot. After some hesitation, and with paws crossed, I puffed my chest out and confidently offered my educated opinion that breeding racoons was a dangerous occupation for any cat, but especially so for a lady Chartreux as elegant, classy and delicate as herself, and not to be recommended, in fact, any manuals on such topic should be banned.

Judging by the incredulous and contemptuous expression on her face, I sensed this was not the synopsis she was quite expecting, with or without *alacrity*. If there had been a 2 metre deep litter tray by the table, I would have happily dived down to the bottom of it.

Thinking that matters could not possibly get any worse, she then asked me what my favourite French novel was.

Was Tin Tin French or Belgian?

Holy Catflaps, can't we just talk about football for five minutes?

My mind raced around faster than a mechanical rabbit on a greyhound track.

At this point, if God had delivered me into the gaping jaws of a rabid Dogue de Bordeaux, this would have resulted in less suffering on my part.

That would have been a merciful release from the bohemian torture I was enduring.

Upon the third time of asking, it was like being interrogated by La Direction Générale de la Sécurité Extérieure, so I volunteered what I hoped would satisfy her literary demands…

With my paws crossed and a lump in my throat so large I was almost garrotted by my collar, I replied: **'Asterix and Obelix: Mission Cleopatra'.**

I promptly shut my eyes and waited to have the contents of her milk saucer poured over my head.

After a couple of minutes, I opened one eye to see that she was looking at me even more incredulously

and contemptuously than before… for what seemed like an eternity. Then she proceeded to laugh out loud whilst stroking my whiskers and complimenting me on my charming wit. Phew. I just sat there relieved that I did not reek of Sterilised French Milk.

For a moment, I thought maybe Asterix and Obelix were two lesser known Musketeers deleted from a Dumas novel or characters from Molière's famous work *Le Bourgeois Gentilhomme* (which I thought in the circumstances was quite apt).

To my eternal amazement, she continued to purr for the rest of the evening that I was the cutest cat she had ever come across… it was true after all what they said about the British Blue's renowned sense of humour, and, ipso facto (a Spanish fashion designer?), I was a refreshing change from the preening, pretentious dilettantes from the $5^{th}$ arrondissement who bored her witless. Merci Asterix!

That night, I curled up in my LHC's flat cap (I was not allowed on the bed, even though it was a low-cost and even lower value, *Cachot de Luxe Group* Hotel... *imagine Colditz with croissants*) and had a sleepless night empathising with Napoléon Bonaparte when he first met the aristocratic Joséphine de Beauharnais. Hitherto, the poshest feline I had ever come across was a particularly snooty Siamese with half an ear missing who resided in a tulip centre near Harrogate and whose MX-5 driving LHC went show jumping.

## April

**Virtual Friends**

Having been bombarded by the admittedly well-meaning Kevin with calls and emails and harangued over every type of draft beer in the Merry Monk - save Hemlock Best Bitter - my LHC had given in to pressure and submitted a profile on a dating website.

Two weeks went by but nothing happened. Zero responses.

Then it started raining.

Perhaps this was just a temporary respite from the heat of March?

I bought my first Émile Zola novel from *Amazon* entitled 'L'Assommoir'. I found it so miserable and depressing that I felt like turning to drink myself.

Another week went by and still no response. There might be many fish in the sea but they were not biting at the bait dangled by this fisherman.

'Maybe I'm better off just taking my chances in the bars, Nelson,' said my forlorn companion, whilst we were both staring at his PC in the hope that this may cause an email to pop out of the blue.

'Great. I'll come with you,' I said eagerly, but he sank my ship or sails... or whatever the expression is.

'You're a downright liability and you've already been barred from The Merry Monk - after you gave the barman some lip.'

I tried to explain that it was the barman who started it, but he wasn't prepared to listen.

*Well... if you don't want me to be there as your chaperone and give my brutally honest opinion - then don't moan if you get involved with an English Lorena Bobbit.*

We went back to staring at the screen.

I did find this strange... do humans really think that someone will jump out of the screen as if they have arrived from a *Star Trek* episode? Knowing his luck he'll get a Klingon Lorena Bobbit popping out.

He was starting to resemble Kevin the Cost Accountant with his 274 friends on *Facebook*.

I did ask Kevin several days earlier when he came round to regale The Lonesome Cowboy with the tales of his latest online conquests why, if he had so many friends, did he spend all of his spare time sitting in front of a computer screen in his spare bedroom (or 'study' as he pompously called his human play pen. But why more study, when he is fully qualified?)

Humans never cease to amaze me. They buy amazing technology and all they do is use it to send imbecilic messages to each other or their *phantom* friends via *Facebook*. Their command of English grammar is worse than that of a 4-year old. It seems *the* definite and indefinite articles have been banned forever --- following is -- example of - moronic conversation on *Facebook*:

'Just putting on wacky Mickey Mouse boxers.'

'What time is it?'

'Should I wear blue tie or red one?'

'Had sugar puffs for breakfast.'

'Flat out at work.'

'Me too. Can't cope.'

'Can't cope with my workload either.'

'Deserve pay rise as I must do work of 3 people. No time to breathe.'

'Everyone else in office just buggers about all day. Work sucks.'

'Been shopping. Special deal on fruit so went bananas.'

17 people *Liked* this comment.

'Tuna sandwich with mayo for lunch.'

'Drinking caffè latte.'

'Cleaned out cat's litter tray.'

Pigs became airborne after this comment.

'Just switched on TV. Now't on. Bored.'

'Anybody remember Zebedee from Magic Roundabout?'

'Who?'

'Can't remember if he was married to Florence.'

'Time for tea. Should I have *Baked Beans* or *Alphabetti Spaghetti?*'

'In Dorset we call tea dinner. LOL.'

'Life without friends is like dinner (from Sussex) of bangers without mash.'

'A life without friends is like a dinner of Cat Master Chef Boeuf Bourguignon with no Jersey cream.

Thank you for being my friend. ☺'

'Ironing underpants'.

8 people *Liked* this comment.

'Took dog for walk. Windy.'

'Is it beer time yet?

'Fed cat. 89 pence for can of Cat Master Chef Lamb Hyderabadi. Utter waste of money.
'P.S. Ungrateful little git wouldn't eat it.'

1 cat did not *Like* this comment.

'Go the Jambos.'

'Hail hail. I hate Coisty.'

One half of Glasgow *Liked* this comment.

'Go the Gers. I hate Lennon.'

The other half of Glasgow *Liked* this comment.

'I hate my cat. Wish he'd buzz off.'

'Is he a bee? LOL!'

54 went hysterical at this comment.

'Nope, he serves no useful purpose whatsoever…'

'I think your cat's quite cute.'

'You don't have to live with him.'

'I could happily murder a pint.'

'I could happily murder Nelson.'

13 people, including 11 Cost Accountants, *Liked* this comment.

'Time for bed said Zebedee.'

'Flossing teeth. Bleeding gums.'

'Night Night.'

This buffoonery goes on for hours every day, especially during winter. Why don't they go out, get together and play football?

At least they exchange pleasant and polite messages on *Facebook* unlike the misanthropes who misuse *Twitter*. Another deplorable trait in humans: socially inept and cowardly scoundrels who hide behind the anonymity of the Internet to be vitriolic, offensive and ill-mannered. If they cannot say anything pleasant or constructive about someone then why say anything at all?

I have concluded that the human race has started to regress and that, paradoxically, the great strides in I.T. communications have caused their interpersonal skills to atrophy. Perhaps staring in front of a computer all day and all evening, every day of the week, every week of the year, leads to early onset dementia? Not content with a 40" Sony TV, a computer, a Smartphone and a laptop, my LHC is now toying with the idea of buying one of those little gadgets that seem to offer a bit more than a mobile phone, but a lot less than a laptop.

Seems a bit pointless to me, but everyone raves about them.

He told me he could look at the screen of his Launch Pad on his lap whilst he is watching TV or a DVD, which did make me wonder if his eyes had taken on the optical dexterity of a chameleon.

Going back to the point that I had raised with Cost Accounting Kevin, surely, I said, it would be more enjoyable to go out and see your friends in person?

His response was something along the lines of there being '…lots of ways to skin a cat, especially a pedigree Smart Alec.'

I think this may have been aimed at me, but I was only asking: I must have posted an incorrect debit in his balance sheet.

Personally, I much prefer romping around outside, even when it's snowing, rather than being curled up on my bean bag dreaming about imaginary friends. You never know who you are going to meet… with the only downside being Staffordshire Bull Terriers, who seem to have a pathological hatred of anything on four legs.

It did make me think that there must be thousands of humans up and down the country sitting alone in their 'studies', night after night, perched avidly in front of their computer screens like salivating canines transfixed by the sight of a tin of Chum.

I had suggested that he join a worthwhile club such as The British Shorthair Cat Club or La Société Chartreux Élevage Féline (the Chartreux Breeding Society) as that could be a nice way of meeting friends - but his response was to mutter to one of his 148 imaginary *Facebook* friends about: 'Nelson being more devious than Machiavelli.'

After *Googling* his name, the only Machiavelli I could find was the 2$^{nd}$ choice left-back for Inter Milan, though there was a Mario Machiavelli who played for Manchester City.

From what I had read about Mario, a night out with him sounded like good fun and much more so than the East Lindum Wold's Maisonettes Annual Dinner in June - as recommended by the wife of another of his friends (a maudlin Mechanical Engineer).

She said it would be a great way to increase his social & business networks with the '...cream of society who really hold the reins of power in the land.'

She added that this information was all very secretive and winked her left eye as she shook her head three times.

'What a strange way of carrying on. Probably been on *Facebook* for too long during the previous evening.' Then it occurred to me…

*Does the Queen know about this, as surely by divine right Her Majesty holds the reins of power?*

So, I assumed that it must be the *SAS* in disguise and thought this could be even more fun than fireworks with Mario. Despite asking as politely as possible and promising on Cub Scout's honour not to upset anyone or steal any smoked salmon or profiteroles, I was not allowed to go on account of being:

a) A Catholic.
b) A Cat.
c) Not owning a dinner suit (which I thought was totally unfair, especially as I own a black faux-silk collar).
d) Not being an upstanding member of the business community (yet they let someone be a member who owned a fish and chip shop in Huddersfield. He must have been in charge of their Catering Corps).

But then my LHC did not meet the criteria detailed in (a) above either.

Then, out of the blue, a message popped up, stating that he had an admirer from Bobbington, which made his eyes widen with elation whilst mine widened even further with shock (she **must** be desperate) and… 'would he like to meet up for a drink?'

Holy Hanky Panky.

I can honestly say that I have never seen such an outburst of joy as he hopped round the room like a 6ft Easter Bunny. He even started being nice to **me**; telling me what a wonderful companion I was and thanking me for all my support. I didn't think I had really gone out of my way to help the networking nincompoop, but I did ask what he would do if she really resided in Haiti? I was not actually being serious but he triple-checked her details to confirm that Bobbington is indeed nowhere near Port-au-Prince.

He then read out to me some of her key details:

1) Attractive.
2) Curvaceous.
3) Weight 'rather not say'.
4) Single.
5) Non-smoker.
6) Very light drinker.
7) Into fitness.
8) Looks do not matter.
9) Occupation: **very senior** management role in the NHS.
10)

*Quick_Matron_*the_ screens_please_1973' was looking for a wealthy gentleman who is on her own intellectual level so she could enjoy a stimulating conversation with somebody rich & sophisticated over dinner and a bottle of French Champagne. 'Manual Workers and Mateus Rosé drinkers need not reply.'

The Bunny hopped over the moon and back and, despite my best efforts to curb his primeval urges, he behaved with the subtlety of a stud cat in a breeding cage, suggesting they meet up the next evening – as it was a Friday.

I did try telling him to pay particular attention to Point #10 and try reading behind the lines… I even lay on top of his keyboard and highlighted point #10 by tapping my paw on the screen - but the lovestruck fool took no notice.

Just before Jonah set off the next evening to have a whale of a time, I offered to go as his chaperone, but he scoffed at my offer with reckless abandon…

'I hardly think I'll be having a drink with an axe murderer! After all, she works for the local health authority.'

'So did Josef Mengele,' was my acidic response, remembering that I had seen that inane picture of innocence on the faces of numerous Tom Cats at the Vets' who were about to have that little operation from which there was no coming back.

Alas, he was not to be deterred from his rendezvous with the Angel of Death.

I curled up on my bean bag, wondering who was going to keep me in the lifestyle to which I had become accustomed or would I henceforth have to fend for myself and catch my own food?

At an ungodly hour, he came in looking the worse for wear, but at least he had not been experimented on (brain not applicable).

I had been dreaming about being back in France, when he strutted into the kitchen with the panache of a slightly inebriated peacock and told me how great the evening had been and I had been fretting over nothing...

'She's only been divorced twice. She drove from Bobbington so only had one glass of wine. She has a Masters Degree in I.T., so she must be highly intelligent. She's obviously got class too as she votes Conservative, owns her own house, drives an Audi TT *and* she insisted that I buy a bottle of the most expensive white wine: a £32 Pouilly Fumé.'

'So, are you seeing the free-loading Fraülein Mengele again?' asked Doubting Thomas the Cat.

'At first she told me over the Entrée that she felt there was no spark between us...'

'I said you should have gone dressed as Guy Fawkes...'

'Very funny, Nelson. I should dress *you* up as Guy Fawkes. As I was saying, the evening suddenly changed when she asked me where I was going on holiday and I replied that I had to do some renovations on my house in France, at which point she perked up and said how much she adored France, "*...a cultural paradise*" she called it, even though she had only ever been to Disneyland in Paris (twice). Or maybe it was just coincidence that having complained about her starter being dull and boring she said that her 12 oz. fillet steak looked divine and it was quite nice of me to pay for dinner. She told me she couldn't make the next two weekends as she was tied up with special meetings each evening, must be to do with her high-up role in the NHS *(the naïve fool…)*, but she wants me to organise a weekend away after that.'

He said that without taking a breath.

I went back to sleep, feeling this was doomed and that I had more chance of seeing Beatrice.

# May

**Les bonnes vacances en France**

It continues to rain in biblical quantities.
It has now rained incessantly for over 40 days and 40 nights yet the water authorities up and down the country still refuse to lift their hosepipe bans. Whatever happened to global warming?
Gave all my Asterix DVDs to my plebeian LHC, who is predictably overjoyed: giving me cause to treat him with even more disdain than before.
Mr Gullible did as he was told and organised a romantic weekend away with Fraülein Mengele to some cheap hotel near Scarborough, as all of the York hotels claimed to be booked out.
Probably knew who was coming.
Despite booking the Honeymoon Suite (as she insisted that she only ever stayed in rooms with a terrace and en-suite Jacuzzi), it had by all accounts not gone as planned. In spite of claiming to be a light drinker, she managed to drink two and a half

bottles of Chilean Cabernet Sauvignon in as many hours over dinner, all the while complaining to the waiters…

'Why can't I have a cigarette with my meal?'

So, she had to retire early, whereupon she was violently ill in bed, then blamed Mr Gullible the Wine Merchant for ruining her evening. She then refused to get back into the bed, until he had changed the sheets. I suggested this form of contraception could be a less eye-watering alternative to neutering, but that didn't go down well. Upon departing the hotel, they were cordially invited never to book a room there again. The male member of the party was quite pleased to hear this, but Fraülein Mengele was less enamoured.

I don't think Florence Nightingale would have totally approved of her response:

'DO YOU KNOW WHO YOU'RE TALKING TO? I'm a Silver Member of the *Cachot de Luxe Hotel Group* Loyalty Scheme, and I've earned 64 Loyalty Points already this year. That is almost enough to earn me 2 fabulous nights in Dunkerque.'

Then she attempted to batter the unfortunate YTS Head Receptionist to death, who was only doing as instructed by the Day Manager (who was by now supporting his junior colleague to the hilt, by hiding behind a 3 foot high Ming Vase) with the dozen red roses that my LHC had bought for the trip… before vomiting over him.

Upon exiting, my LHC could hear the vomit-covered YTS Head Receptionist mumbling: "I am going to give up cannabis, work hard and re-sit my A Levels so that I can get into University and get far away from this job…"

So… it transpired that the Fraülein was a Media Relations Officer who was in the middle of her 3rd divorce and owed £260,000 on her house that had recently been valued at £245,000 'if you're lucky.' according to her 5th estate agent.

So, it was back to the drawing board (or a lucky escape) - depending on one's point of view.

Being grateful that she had not moved in, I told him to: '…put it down to experience. What doesn't kill you will only serve to make you stronger…'

I think that's what it said on the back of a pretty, but overly-tattooed Bajan singer, who had posed for a photo shoot in *Laddo* Magazine next to: 'Let he who has not sinned, cast the first pebble',  that sounds like the kind of thing Winston would say.

With a steely determination of which Scipio would have been proud, he decided to persevere, largely because he made a mistake and ticked the box for the 12-month subscription instead of the 1-month choice.

A week later, his perseverance paid off as gets in touch with someone who is…

'Dying to meet up for a quiet drink and see if there is any chemistry'.

Perhaps she is a science teacher? I suggested that he organise a barbecue, so that she could bring her bunsen burner, but my little comment got me booted outside.

Mmmm, it seems that she is another non-smoking, light drinking, gym bunny. By now, I had a recurring feeling of déjà vu.

'Just be careful out there. Don't meet up in a dark alley and make sure you keep your mobile on.'

I advised him, but knew that he would not listen to a word I said. He always does the opposite of what I advise. Typical human... got a mind of his own.

Around midnight, I was lying back on my bean bag listening to Herbie Hancock, when just as *Can't tell who Island* was about to play, the front door opened and he burst into the kitchen to tell me he had enjoyed a wild evening with a 15st 7lb social worker called Charity who '...was blessed with the face of an Angel.'

'Sounds like she was blessed with the body of a Botticelli Angel.'

At this point, the clearly worse for wear Botticelli Angel sailed into the kitchen.

'Are you calling me fat?' she asked Romeo.

'No, I just...'

'I've spent 10 weeks on the *Atkins Diet* and have lost 11 lbs already. I look **fantastic** - don't you agree?'

I was going to mention that it was difficult to say, due to the voluminous black top and trousers that she was wearing... in fact, she could have passed for a Political Commissar for the Khmer Rouge *Weight Watchers*. But I lay motionless on my bean bag, not daring to say a word - in case she sat on me.

'Would you like a caipirinha?'

'A what... does it have vodka in it? I only drink vodka - not any o' that foreign muck.'

My heart sank quicker than the Euro... *I hope she's not staying the night.* Then, to my unbridled horror, her bloodshot eyes met mine. It was loathing at first sight.

'Urrgh, what's that furry blue thing doing on that big whoopee cushion?

'Let me introduce you to my loyal little feline companion Nelson...'

'I hate cats. Diabolical creatures. Got attacked by one once.'

'What did it do, grab you by the throat?'

By this time, even Herbie had stopped singing.

'Charity, how about you sit in the lounge, whilst I make your drink. He's not a totally stupid cat. In fact, I have taught him how to help me make caipirinhas. Why don't you just bend down, say hello and stroke his head for a minute? He loves that.'

'If she comes anywhere near me, I'm going to bite her curvaceous hand off.' I declared, shuffling backwards.

'You must be joking. I hate cats. They ruin your curtains, spray everywhere and kill all the wildlife. I mean, when's the last time you saw a sparrow?'

'Maybe that's due to their natural predators: sparrowhawks?'

'A sparrowhawk? Never heard of them. Don't be so stupid and **don't argue with me.** They should be locked up at 6 p.m. every night. We had a pet cat once, but I was allergic to it, so I had it put down.'

'That's a bit extreme isn't it? Did its death cure your allergy?'

**'I** think so… but I was told by my useless GP that he thought it was either hayfever or dust mites. So I changed doctors.'

Is she really a social worker??

He seems smitten with her, so she stays the night, after I had been asked to be nice to her and take no notice of any insensitive comments - as she is quite a warm-hearted person…

'Such… as she sneezed one day, so she had her cat executed.' I suggested this seemed a tad cold-hearted to me.

Maybe she is more relaxed when she hasn't drunk a bottle of vodka, although the pair of them looked like *death warmed up* when they surfaced at midday.

In an attempt to win her over, I went out at daybreak and managed to catch a sparrow, which I thought would be a nice gift for her, even though its head fell off when I dragged it through my flap. So, I dropped its body into one of her knee-length leather boots and its head into the other - as mementoes of her first visit to our house.

It was Sunday afternoon and I was lying on the leather sofa in the salon (he calls it his lounge) reading *The Economist* whilst relaxing with some Chet Baker in the background, when they finally stumbled downstairs. They both complained of feeling terrible and she needed a cigarette or two and 'hair of the dog' whatever that is. She had admitted drinking half a bottle of vodka before she met him then a full bottle of vodka during the evening, along with smoking 20 cigarettes. With her curly blonde hair and harsh features (they were probably due to the pressure of being a social worker) she could have passed for Medusa's binge-drinking sister.

She sat down on the sofa with such a thud that I shot up 18-inches into the air. To my delight, she said that she had to go home as she was feeling really squeamish and she might be ill at any moment. So, in an obsequious attempt to appear (uncharacteristically) gallant, Casanova offered to take her home straightaway. I'm sure that this had nothing to do with him being concerned that she might change the colour scheme of his recently arrived, handmade, Chinese rug. Similarly, I was also concerned that I may not be a British Blue for much longer.

She ordered *Parker* to wait a minute as she had to go into the hall to put on her knee-length leather boots which had cost her a fortune at *Hervé Rix*...

when I remembered there were two little presents awaiting her.

I buried my head in a cushion and waited for her screams… but there was nothing.

'Hmm, perhaps she has collapsed?' I wondered. 'Or maybe she has finally entered a comatose state?'

The calm was shattered as she barked at *Parker* about being ready to go and she wanted him to take her via the supermarket, as she needed some milk, cheddar and cigarettes.

I was tempted to ask if she would be so kind as to buy some *Cat Master Chef,* but felt her response might be to cover me in whatever she had gurgling inside her stomach.

They drove off into the supermarket-beckoning sunset and I went back to reading about what the future held for France under the new Socialist President Hollande.

When *Parker* came back, later that evening, he said that the boots (£285) didn't seem to fit her properly any more and had a foul smell emanating

from them - so she was taking them back and demanding a full refund.

He then told me that earlier that morning, when I was outside on my 3 km run, he had booked us onto *Eurotunnel* and we were off to France next week for ten days holiday. Hurrah!

However, my whiskers drooped when he informed me that his latest amour: the vodka-swilling, cat murdering, unsociable social worker would also be coming by plane the day after we arrive - so I was under the strictest orders '…not to misbehave and to make her feel welcome - unlike the last one…' who I apparently upset by curling up and going to sleep on her head at 2:00 a.m. when she had retired for the evening.

As far as I was concerned, she was in my bed (he always tells me that he never has enough space in the car to pack my bean bag, but I am quite content with this compromise as a double bed is much more to my liking).
She should have slept on the sofa.

The drive down to Folkestone was rather tiresome, especially when we got to a road called the M25, which I presumed must refer to its maximum speed limit. However, the trip through the tunnel (under the sea) was great fun.

We stopped at a charming chambre d'hôte near Neufchâtel-en-Bray, run by a delightful English couple, where I was given the same food as all the humans - apart from melon and wine. Whilst everyone had a pre-dinner aperitif, I had time to go for a run along a footpath, which was formerly a railway line (to Dieppe) and I inspected the local château. Trotting past all of the ancient, pretty, half-timbered houses, I thought that I could easily live here, and even change my name to de Lapérouse, but then the heavens opened up and I got soaked… so I changed my mind.

On the drive out of Neufchâtel-en-Bray the next morning, we stopped at the best supermarket I have ever been in. Half of Monsieur Leclerc's store was dedicated to produce sold by the local farmers. Being a typical *homme anglais*, he just raved about the cider and Calvados, whilst I focused on the local meat, cheese and cream.

Seven hours later, we arrived at the maison and he insisted, as usual, that I go in first to check it out for des souris, rats, frelons et serpents, then let him know when it was safe to come in.

After I had given *Rick Attenborough* the all clear - though there were a dozen dead frelons by the fireplace - he boldly entered where no rosbif had entered before... at least since the previous summer.

Having opened up the house, we sat back to watch Mésrine Part I, with a pizza and a Jenlain Ambrée / milk.

It was whilst Jacky Mésrine was robbing his first bank that my LHC informed me that unsociable Charity was indeed allergic to cats as she had been violently ill at the cheese counter at *Maurice and Sons,* which she said had proved her point '...so don't you or your clever little cat ever question me again'.

'So... nothing to do with the fact that she drank more vodka than a Cossack Cavalry Regiment the previous night?'

I suggested, just as Mésrine shot his first victim.

He informed me that I need to keep my distance, otherwise her eyes will swell up and she will start sneezing uncontrollably. This sounds like superb free entertainment to me and much more fun than watching *The English Patient* on DVD for the fifth time.

Of course, it doesn't occur to him that I might be allergic to *her,* especially if she tries to pick me up and calls me Puss and comments on the size of my jowels (a male feature of my clan), sans ironie, bearing in mind her statuesque physique.

I am press-ganged into going with him the next day to Limoges Airport and admire the scenery of the Limousin, thinking that I could have a field day chasing rodents and rabbits in the woods and fields.

We arrived at the airport, where she was waiting with what seemed like enough suitcases to sink the Titanic and wearing the same leather boots from the previous weekend. She was in a bad mood as we were 45 minutes late. My LHC apologetically told her that we were stuck behind a tractor for most of the journey, but that failed to placate her. I interjected and told her, as diplomatically as possible, that if she didn't like France and all of its charming quirks, then she shouldn't have come and she still had time to get the *Harp Air* flight back to Leeds Bradford Airport. I even offered to help push her suitcases back to the check-in area. At which point, my LHC gripped my jaws so tightly I could have been auditioning for *The Man In The Iron Mask*. With widening eyes, and even puffier jowels than usual, I tried to intimate that I could barely breathe or purr - let alone speak.

So my perfidious *not-so-LHC* butted in and apologised obsequiously for… 'the unsympathetic behaviour and appalling, ill-mannered attitude of my pet cat.'

I had to assume this was a reference to me.

Had I been able to swivel my head, I would have looked around to see if there were any other felines in sight.

*Non, c'était moi...* I could feel the fur standing up on my back but was undecided as to whether this was due to struggling to breathe, cringing with embarrassment or being annoyed at:

1. Him trying to appease her with his pathetic apologies.
2. Him referring to me as his 'pet cat'.
3. Her asking him: 'Do you really expect me to share your car with *that cat* sat on my lap?'

He then let go and I collapsed onto the tarmac with outstretched legs, as though I had pre-death rigor mortis. As I struggled to regain full consciousness I could hear - in the foggy mist of my oxygen-starved mind - the not very serene social worker Charity berating him in the dulcet Lancastrian tone reminiscent of the woman in the *Boddington's Beer* TV ad – along the lines of...

'That disgusting cat, who I would like to kill, put a dead bird in my boots. *Hervé Rix* refused to give me a refund on the grounds that there was the body of a semi-eviscerated sparrow in the left boot, and its decapitated head in the right...'

She had complained so loudly in *Hervé Rix* that two Baristas had come flying down from the top floor faster than steam out of a *Gaggia* to see if someone had been murdered.

She had demanded of the unfortunate sales assistant, who had just won that month's Store Award for providing 'Platinum Quality Customer

Service', that she cancel her *Hervé Rix* Loyalty Card forthwith and... 'No, she did not want a complimentary \*\*\*\*\*\*\* Double \*\*\*\*\*\*\* Espresso' before being escorted out of the building, ranting and raving in a manner unbecoming of a social worker...

'I spent £16.75 on a *Vespa*-riding priest mug, plus a bag of decaf *Hervé Rix* own label coffee last month and this is the way you treat one of your loyal customers. From now on I'm going to give all my custom to House of Frazier...'

So she ordered that **he** should pay for the cost of her flight as he was vicariously culpable. If I had been physically capable I would have told her that the sparrow was only ever intended to be a little peace offering.

By now, I had managed to stand up and, having narrowly missed being run over by a *Hertz*-rented *Citroën Picasso* driven by an estate agent from Ajaccio, was about to reply to point #3 raised by the ungrateful gorgon: from my own perspective, I would sooner dive into a pool of crocodiles than sit on her lap. Plus, she should be grateful for the kind offer of a free holiday (excluding the flight)... but he again covered my mouth and unceremoniously hurled me into the back seat.

On the drive back to Montmorillon, he perfected the art of grovelling, whilst I nursed my wounded pride on his Royal Stewart Tartan Rug in the back seat - and was mesmerised by its vivid colour scheme. She continued to make caustic comments at my expense, to the point that I was tempted to roll up the rug, put a knot in one end then garrotte her with it, but decided that this may not go down too well on his Internet dating profile.

He seemed emotionally and psychologically battered already and we had only just picked her up. What was the rest of the week going to be like? She didn't look like the kind of girl who would be up for a game of *Scalectrix* over a Chimay Rouge/sterilised milk. Needless to say, the mood in the car was about as animated, ribald and cheery as Comedy Night at a Trappist Monastery.

As we approached Montmorillon, he perked us up by saying, as a special treat, he had booked us all in for Sunday lunch at the Hôtel de Strasbourg - which was the main reason for our tardy arrival at the airport. I did not remember him driving via the Hôtel de Strasbourg on the way to the airport - so wondered if I had under-estimated his powers of telepathy.

This also explained why I got the double flea and worming treatment earlier that morning and I almost felt guilty for 'half-severing three of his fingers' (the usual hyperbole on his part) - whilst he was administering said medication. I remembered he had made me wear a ridiculous cat collar decorated with alternating paw prints and red hearts which he bought from the local hypermarket. Had he enrolled me on a lonesome moggy dating site too? Alas no... it was simply to impress his new, implacable amour who had reiterated on their second date in an Indian Restaurant (I tried telling him he needs to be more imaginative) that she hated cats and this could lead to relationship-breaking problems between them **if they were ever to move in together**.

'**MOVE IN TOGETHER**....???'

I could feel my copper eyes getting wider by the minute at this horrendous thought. How about someone asking me for my opinion in these delicate negotiations? I thought about writing to *The Cats Protection Societies* of both France and the UK, telling them about my impending dual evictions.

If he could get rid of her, perhaps by telling her that I have rabies (I would happily go along with this by foaming at the mouth and rolling around the floor *impersonating one of his previous drunken Internet dates...* or a particularly virulent strain of Asian Cat Anthrax Flu)... I would solemnly promise to never moan again about dry cat food, nor resist being wormed.

Sorry... I digress.

We arrived at the car park opposite the Hotel and, had I been laying in a plant-pot full of catmint I couldn't have been in a more euphoric state as I dreamed about eating Coquilles Saint Jacques for both a starter and main course, followed by crème brulée.

She actually stopped moaning as we walked into the restaurant of the Hôtel de Strasbourg, which was full of septuagenarian French widows (or more likely divorcees) fawning over their stupid toy dogs. Neither use nor ornament in my opinion - with their vacuous expressions as if premature dementia had set in (the dogs, that is...).

I spotted a sign at the entrance to the restaurant stating: 'Chiens bienvenus. Interdit aux chats.' which I felt was rather absurd and discriminatory. So much for la liberté, la fraternité et l'égalité…

Before I could say :
'Excusez-moi garçon, je voudrais commander des Coquilles Saint Jacques s'il vous plaît…' a waiter (who will never get my vote for the Award of Poitou-Charentes Maître d'Hôtel of the Year) grabbed hold of me by my jewel-encrusted collar (if that was offending him so much, I would have been more than happy to take it off) and slung me into the adjoining, and much less salubrious, 'Le Marchand' bar next door.

I dusted myself down, with as much dignity as I could in the circumstances, to find that I was being stared at by a bunch of pie-eyed, ex-pat British humans, each of whom looked like they had just drunk more Absinthe in the past 3 hours than Toulouse Lautrec had consumed in his entire life. I noticed a scribbled menu on the wall offering 'Le plat du jour: omelette au jambon avec des frites: €12'.

Now, I may not have been studying French for three years at night school, but my command of the language was sufficient to know that this clearly was not a Michelin-starred eatery.
It was an unusual bar by French standards as it featured an *Elvis* Tribute Band singing: '*Hound Dog*' which did sound odd being sung in English with a rural French accent.

The singer had the biggest sideburns I had ever seen, though I am not sure sandals with jeans were quite in keeping, nor his hi-viz jacket with 'Commune de Montmorillon' printed on the back.

He did look remarkably like one of the dustmen who once accused me of ripping into all the bin bags at the public area for poubelles. I asked him if he had ever seen a fox before, but he looked at me with the vacant expression of someone who was chronically in-bred.

I assumed the song must have been dedicated to another septuagenarian French lady's toy poodle that was sitting under the table near me.

Given the vacuous expression on its face and its rolling tongue, it was obviously oblivious to being serenaded. It looked like one of Pavlov's dogs that had been given a day off, but still could not stop salivating at the thought of food; probably because it was transfixed by her plate of moules marinières. Then I witnessed something truly awful: she placed a mussel in her mouth, bent down, and encouraged the dog to take it from her… **using its own mouth**.

Urrgh, disgusting. I had a good mind to complain to the Bar Owner but he was too busy banging on the drums for the French Elvis.

I was pondering how to get back into the Hotel restaurant, when I was hit on the head with a huge, overcooked frite and asked by the drunken, aspiring Team GB javelin thrower: 'Oi. Do yer like ketchup on yer chips, fleabag???'

His fellow Neanderthal drinking companions thought the quip of this modern-day Oscar Wilde to be wildly hysterical and were laughing and pointing at me. Drunken moggies.

So, I picked up the frite and threw it back at him, but missed, and instead hit his wife's 250ml glass of red wine, knocking it over. The contents spilt onto her new, white *Pierre Cardin* dress and a big, leather bag that was nestled in her lap.

She glowered at him, so he truculently explained: 'It's that cat's fault. He threw it at me.'

His erstwhile drinking companions slowly withdrew to a safe distance - behind a 2CV belonging to the bass-playing Sapeur-Pompier.

She shot her Medusa-like gaze towards me, so my immediate Pavlovian reaction was to adopt a yoga-like seated pose with all four legs tucked under my stomach, looking like le *Beurre du Président* butter would not melt in my mouth. Being a coward of the lowest order, as well as a flat-track bully, he aimed a sly kick at me, but with my inherent reactions, I was able to nimbly skip over his boot.

With a mounting rage, akin to an emotional heat wave spreading through her veins, she shouted:

'Don't be so stupid. Do yer take me for a complete fool? **A CHIP-THROWING CAT???** You'll be telling me next that it can speak French too!'

Then she slapped him so hard across the chops that he flew off his chair and, on his downward trajectory, gave a headbutting coup de grâce to the unfortunate, mussel-munching hound dog.

The mercurial Montmorillon ex-pat gin queen's answer to Bruce Lee was clearly not to be trifled with, as she started to bash him over his head with her newly burgundy-dyed handbag screaming: 'Do you know how much this *Louis \*\*\*\*\*\*\* Vuitton* handbag cost me…?'

By this time, he was unable to offer an answer, being semi-comatose and half-battered to death.

' …€1,995 from their ******* flagship store on the ******* Champs-Élysées.'

Which sounded rather a lot to me, when I considered how much my cat litter tray cost.

I decided to beat a hasty retreat, before she turned her implacable wrath upon me, but not before suggesting she would have been better spending her money on a thesaurus. Or in her case, a ******* thesaurus.

This did little to assuage her anger, bearing in mind how many *Kronenbourg* beer glasses and *Ricard* ashtrays came flying my way, as I found my inner-cheetah and sprinted over the bridge in the direction of Pindray, home and sanctuary.

As I did so, the recently bereaved owner of the now defunct hound dog started screaming insults at Mme. Louis ****** *Vuitton* and threw her carafe of red wine at her; adding further colour to the formerly white frock and covering three of her friends from Essex… who had all been enjoying the first day of their summer holidays, in the friendly, serene and relaxing paradise that is rural France.

Then it all kicked off, as those husbands who had not been half-bludgeoned to death joined in. The old adage occurred to me that the best entertainment in life is always free…

When I reached the *Vélo-Sport* shop I decided that I was out of projectile range, so felt it safe to turn around for an instant to see what was happening. It could have been the Fourth Battle of Poitiers.

Mme. \*\*\*\*\*\*\* *Vuitton* was going berserk (the Vikings would have been proud of her and I was half-tempted to go back to tell her she could always get a job as a part-time tour guide at the *Jorvik Centre* in York…). She was wielding her handbag above her head like a medieval ball on a chain (had it been 1356, the Black Prince would have signed her up for his European tour) whist I could see *Elvis* restraining one of the wine-splattered Essex Girls in a headlock, shouting at her to shut up and calm down.

He definitely wasn't singing *'Love Me Tender'*. This gave a new meaning to Mr Presley's famous expression 'Thank you, ma'am. Uh huh.'

Meanwhile, the Bar Owner who was ruminating: 'Et je croyais que Jeanne d'Arc était une cinglé.' ('And I thought Joan of Arc was a nutter.') - had sought sanctuary behind his drum kit and proved so highly adept at deflecting beer glasses with two cymbals that he could get a position as reserve percussionist with the *Limoges Philharmonic Orchestra.*

I carried on home, barely noticing the van full of Gendarmes flying past in the opposite direction.

The next day, as I was performing my early morning stretches, I heard my LHC again trying to placate the sullen Charity who was complaining that the nearest beach was 120 kilometres away at La Rochelle. I later found out that their meal was a disaster, as he did not know what gésiers were, but had assured her they would be a culinary delight, as it was a superb restaurant deserving of at least one *Michelin* star.

Unfortunately, she found his *Book of French Culinary Terms* when they got back to notre maison and he had highlighted '**gésiers**' in pink along with '**ris de veau**' and '**tête de veau**'. Even she was able to deduce that pink was not ideal for a Rosbif, though she had said during lunch that her **'cervelle en beignet'** was 'exquisite and almost as good as a tikka masala'. It seems the females of both species can at times be so capricious.

She then complained - with an admittedly impressive *Duracell* bunny-like stamina - that she was bored witless being stuck in the middle of nowhere (I ventured to argue that I did not think that was possible) so I suggested she should venture to 'Le Marchand' where a sense of ennui would have been welcome relief for the owner - after the events of the previous day.

However... the mood à Chez Nelson did not improve.

The next evening we walked/loped the 2 kilometres to the fabulous Belgian Bar 'Le Paradis des Trappistes' in Montmorillon. This event expanded our knowledge of the French Language as my LHC was informed by Charity that Gauloise Ambrée should actually be pronounced GAZ WAZ. Even the French barman didn't know this. This may explain why it took so long for my LHC's 'Gaz Waz' beer to arrive, preceded by the entire staff of the bar coming over to our table, specifically to inform le stupide Rosbif that '... they proudly stocked over 200 Belgian Beers but not one called La bière Gaz Waz.'

Before finally embarking on a sneezing fit, Charity regally announced that she had had enough and wanted to fly back to England, where she could concentrate on meeting someone who owned an apartment that was situated somewhere hotter, classier and less boring... such as Ibiza.

When he dropped her off at Limoges Airport, he felt mightily relieved that the ordeal was over, but as she went to check in, she found out that the next flight to Leeds Bradford Airport was two days later. By this time he was driving along the N147 back to Montmorillon.

When she rang his mobile to order him to turn around, she did not know that he had left his mobile at Chez Nelson and the person who eventually answered her fourth text, having deleted her three voicemail messages, was moi.

After wondering whether to just ignore this barrage of increasingly irate messages, I decided to consider her sad plight, so I sent her the following text:

Chaz, u said it was me or the cat... **BON VOYAGE**. LOL

Followed, for a bit of merriment, by:

PS Hôtel Cachot de Luxe in Limoges supposed 2 b very nice LOL encore!

And then:

PPS Nelson asked if u visit porcelain factory shop, plz get im nice milk saucer.

I then decided it might be in my own best interests to delete these messages and her number. Upon which, I switched off his mobile. When he got back, I was busy practising boules in the garden with my ping pong balls when he came over to join me with *Nina Simone* playing on his MP3/mobile phone.

'That's strange…' he said. 'The ring tone on my mobile has changed to Nina Simone singing about her baby caring only for her.

'Really? I wondered how that could have happened… perhaps Charity changed it for you?'

He then commented that he had received 37 bile-ridden text messages from someone he had never heard of threatening violence towards the pair of us - involving smashing an entire set of dinner plates over our heads.

'You've got to be careful and maintain your guard at all times. It's a jungle out there, you really don't know what types of psychos might be out to get you. Can you think of anyone whom you might have upset recently?

'No, not at all. I haven't done anything to upset anybody.'

'Wasn't signed J. Mésrine was it??'
'Err, no. I thought the French Cops killed him in 1979?'

'That's what they say, but he was a master of disguise - so who knows whether that was him?'

I eventually managed to dissuade the panic-stricken member of our boules contest from informing the Gendarmes and instead he deleted the texts - but made sure that he closed all the shutters that evening. However, he did lie awake all night wondering who on earth would want to murder him…

I slept like a log.

Meanwhile, the remainder of our holiday was a much more relaxing time with him deciding, after several years of procrastinating, that he wanted to buy a road bike. So he placed a deposit on a brand new *Bianchi* bike, which would be ready for collection later in the summer.

# June

**Salieri, Mozart and the Frelons**

It is the Queen's Jubilee Celebrations. It continues to rain cats and dogs (or so I am told, though I haven't spotted any airborne Corgis) but this does little to dampen the nation's spirits which may not be unrelated to the fact that everyone, even every member of the Labour Party, is given an extra day's holiday.

Now I realise why Australia will never become a republic.

This is a portrait of my new French copine, the one whom I met in March, pigeon hunting in the Montparnasse Cemetery. She sent me this out-of-the-blue. A beautiful and well-bred (flea-free) Chartreuse called - and I hesitate to say this on account of the anticipated sniggering and guffawing - Fanny.

To all of you francophobic comedians out there, I would just like to say that Fanny is a very popular name in France. I am conscious that the sniggering and guffawing will have now increased to a deafening crescendo, so I would like to say, to anyone who is still paying attention, that Fanny is actually an abbreviation of STEPHANIE.

No wonder she doesn't want to visit the Yorkshire Dales…

### Nelson the Cat: Guest of Honour at The East Lindum Wolds Maisonettes Annual Dinner

Casanova had, in another moment of reckless abandon, booked two tickets for himself and the sozzled social worker for the East Lindum Wolds

Maisonettes Annual Dinner to be held in a rural town called Bleakborough-on-the-Wolds which was situated in – according to the *AA* Road Map - the middle of nowhere.

His latest romance had lasted about as long as Adolf Hitler's marriage to Eva Braun… and now he was stuck with a spare ticket to the event. He felt that he would have been the laughing stock of every fish n' chip owning Maisonette in Lincolnshire had he gone alone, so guess who was asked, having previously been told that he was unwanted?

*We* went with Bob and Moana Maudlin (a Mechanical Engineer and his wife) plus their Scottish friend, a very nice lady called Kristen, whose philandering husband had run off a month earlier with his Personal Assistant. They were now to be found living in a love nest in Arbroath, which I assumed must be renowned north of the border as a venue for romantic weekends.

After pre-dinner drinks, we were assigned to Table 5, and joined by Guiseppe and Bev Salieri, a charming Anglo-Italian couple who both loved opera. Despite having entertained dreams of playing lead cello at the *Royal Opera House,* Bev had settled for the next best occupation as a Panel Beater (the auto trade's equivalent of a timpanist) in the nearby market town of Ribald-upon-Trent. This was a very successful career choice, probably due to the erratic standard of driving in North Nottinghamshire villages - especially after closing time on Fridays - and the profits had enabled her to give free cello lessons to the inmates at the nearby Rumbunch Prison.

Her husband had emigrated from Italy in 1967 with his parents and had built up a successful taxi business and shuttle service to the *East Midlands Airport*. But his passion in life was opera, especially Mozart, and he had spent the last 22 years trying to get the *Ribald-upon-Trent Opera Company & Philharmonic Orchestra* up and running. They had managed to purchase a derelict warehouse - named it *La Scala* - and conducted several performances: although 18 members of the 21-piece orchestra were cellists.

After eating the main course, they disappeared to lead the *Combined East Midlands Maisonettique & HMP Rumbunch Inmates Orchestra* in playing a succession of operatic compositions - ranging from Don Giovanni to The Marriage of Figaro. Salieri seemed so proud to be conducting the music it was as though he had chosen to forsake all of life's other pleasures for his music.

Unfortunately, their enthusiasm was not matched by the quality of the music – plus 4 of the 9 HMP Rumbunch Members of the orchestra failed to return after the first interlude.

*I assumed they must have resigned… people don't give much notice nowadays.*

The orchestra seemed to get worse the more they drank and their rendition of '**Non più andrai'** was so dire it was as though Salieri had stripped out half the notes.

By the time they had started to eviscerate 'The Requiem', death would have been a merciful release…

'Salieri really did murder Mozart', I sighed, with a heavy heart.

The Scottish lady had also booked two tickets, so her unfortunate situation was the object of much ill-mannered innuendo and mirth by the other 'honourable guests'.

I find mocking other people's misfortunes to be an ignoble trait peculiar to humans, making me grateful to be a feline. The 'honourable guests' didn't seem very honourable to me – they were mocking this unfortunate lady whilst quaffing pint after pint of the locally brewed Supreme Being Top Dog Best Bitter with their haute cuisine meal of scampi and chips.

'Never slow to make a quick buck these Maisonette Chippies…' I thought, with a sour taste in my mouth.

However, she showed admirable stoicism in the face of their cruel and mocking comments (stoicism is a most admirable trait, common in Scotties… Rex, not the dog). So, I tried to cheer her up by engaging in conversation. When she asked me why I had come down all the way from Yorkshire with my LHC (who was becoming even more maudlin than Bob the Maudlin Mechanical Engineer), I didn't want to tell her the truth - so just came out with the first thing I could think of…

'I felt it my duty to show my support for freeing Maison from jail - having assumed he is a relative of Nelson Mandela.'

Kristen had a loud chuckle over that, then told me

how much she loved The Specials and how much she had been dreading coming along on her own - as her philandering husband was well known to the pig breeding gentry and takeaway tycoons east of Doncaster.

Then a pork pie munching, beer-swilling Maisonette Pig Farmer on Table 6 complained that comments like that were totally uncalled for and he would ask his Worshipful Emperor to eject me if I: '…continued with any inappropriate wisecracks - like that one'. I was tempted to reply that I felt it was not unreasonable for Kristen and I to expect to conduct a private conversation inside the temple of a secret society.

Five minutes later, I was sitting outside with half a bowl of scampi and a pork sausage. This was due to an innocent question from a non-worshipper. I just mentioned that I was looking forward to a post-dinner game of chess with him on the giant chessboard in the middle of the hall, so would he mind moving the giant chess pieces as they would be too big for me? It was not as though I was asking him to be my personal Steward. His immediate response was to eject me.

I felt I had been castled.

On my way out, assuming I would never again be invited to dinner in their Lodge, I did manage to ask some valedictory questions:

'Why is everyone running around with their trouser legs rolled up? Is it some arcane ritual connected to fraternal frolicking?' To which I got a stonewall response. Can I replicate your handshake with my paw? 'Could…'

'Booga off and **don't ever** come back,' was the worshipful response, albeit not the zenith of fraternal friendship.

So, I was outside on my own in the dark (in a howling gale), ruminating on the consequences of having ruined my chances of being the first British Blue to become a Maisonette Bleu and have my own Cat Lodge. Luckily, I could cope with the howling gale and driving rain, due to my plush coat, which really makes me waterproof...

*'Summer in England where it never stops raining. No wonder so many humans here want to emigrate. It's such a shame that the inventiveness of the English, the game of cricket for example, is not rewarded with a more clement climate.'* I thought to myself.

Five minutes later, Kristen was similarly exiled from the Maisonette Serfdom, on account of laughing too loud at what I had said and giving them what she felt was a taste of their own flea drops. She also had suggested a place where the self-important occupant on Table 6 could shove his sausages - with gay abandon...

So... we had a very nice chat until 'the carriages' arrived at 1.00 a.m. I was expecting horses and cabs, but all that arrived were some gleaming new *Fiat 500s* with 'Salieri's Worshipful Taxis' written on the sides.

It occurred to me that she could have been a nice lassie for my LHC, but she went off before I had the opportunity to introduce him to her. He had not even spoken to her, as he had to endure listening to the maudlin Mechanical Engineer: '...pompously drone on all night about Wave Energy. I have never been so bored in all my life.'

At least with social worker Charity a dull night would never have been on the cards.

Wave Energy seemed quite an interesting concept to me, though I didn't see how I could generate much energy by waving my paws - but he informed me that he was referring to waves in the sea. I was bored already…

### Les frelons en France

My LHC got an email from France telling him there may be problems with hornets in the house, as lots of people were getting them. As it was also the music festival in Montmorillon, he decided to pop over for a few days, taking myself and one of his mates from Sunderland – this chap had just broken up with his girlfriend, who had been with him for 16 years. Apparently, she was looking for more commitment but: '…he wasn't ready for that yet and didn't want her to move in with him.'

I was tempted to say that had he left it much longer they might be moving into the same burial plot.

As it was just a short trip, my LHC paid for us to fly with *Harp Air*; assuming they had not closed down the LBA to Limoges route after their experiences with an irate, vodka-fuelled social worker who insisted on smoking.

The flights were exceedingly good value at £89 each return - plus a paltry £126 per person/cat in taxes.

I was greatly looking forward to the flight, until a pedantic *Harp Air* checkout harpy ordered us to

**HALT** and announced: 'The cat is not allowed to have a seat. *It* will have to go in the hold.'

'But how can I put it in the hold, when I haven't brought the cat carrier with me? It's too late to pop home and pick it up.'

'You should have thought of that. But you will be pleased to know that you can buy one of our own *Harp Air* Cat Carriers at a highly-competitive rate of £35 each...'

'**£35???** Ok, I suppose I've got no choice. Are you listening to this Nelson?' He said resentfully, as though it was my fault.
'Plus... you have to pay a Cat Tax.'

**'A Cat Tax?'** exclaimed the incredulous Booze Brothers (I was too disgusted to say anything).

'Yes, a cat tax. That will be £20 each way - plus an insurance charge of 25%.'

'Is there anything else you'd like to charge us for? Perhaps there is a sitting down tax or a breathing tax or a using the onboard toilet tax?'

'There is no need to be clever with me, sir... I am just doing my job. Remember that we are still the cheapest carrier and, now that you mention it, we are contemplating charging passengers a fee of £1 or €1 every time they use the onboard toilet facilities. We recently ran a dozen focus groups across the UK and Ireland with a total of 72 customers...'

'What, and they actually liked the idea of paying to use the loo?'

'No, they hated it, so we ignored their worthless opinions and we have since blacklisted the research agency, Uttabollox Insight, who were clearly incompetent amateurs.'

'Great. Any more charges or taxes?'

'Well... it can get very cold in the hold, so we recommend that you buy one of our thermal bean bags which fit snugly inside our *Harp Air* Cat Carriers. It only costs £29.95. Plus cats are more likely to suffer from dehydration, so we recommend some mineral water and UHT sterilised milk - the combined cost is a really good value £4.95. These fit in two, separate, little bowls which are built into the cat carrier.'

'And how much do they cost?'

'These are complimentary, sir.'

By this time, I was checking out the last minute deals to Islamabad with *PIA*.... but he paid his fees and I was incarcerated in the cat carrier. I had the indignity of sharing the flight with 51 fishing rods and 18 sets of golf clubs.
To add to my unhappiness, the owners of the fishing rods were members of the Cobblewaithe-upon-Dale Fly Fishing Club who sarcastically wished me a pleasant flight.

I have to say they looked utterly ridiculous in their camouflage outfits, so I could not help commenting:

'I did not realise that the *SAS* had its own fishing club, but wouldn't shades of blue be a more appropriate colour scheme - unless you are hoping to catch those French fish that like to get out of the water, shake themselves down then go jogging or cycling along the riverbank for 20 kms?

Perhaps these are the rare truites du triathlon?'

After which, I sat in my cat carrier and, with a friendly smile, waved a regal paw at them as I disappeared down the baggage chute. I believe their replies were so abusive that three of them were accused by the *Harp Air* Harpy of pre-flight air rage - so were barred from the flight.

The flight itself was uneventful; the cat carrier was actually quite comfortable.

We duly landed in Limoges, where one of our ex-pat, rosbif friends had kindly arranged to pick us up. He had a special treat for us the next day, which was Clay Pigeon Shooting in Poitiers. Unfortunately, they didn't have any shotguns my size, but I was told that I was welcome to come along and his wife would cook us a barbecue, including fresh sardines (now that would make a pleasant change from dry cat food).

Dennis had told us that the pollen count was very high and to be extremely wary of frelons - at which point, my idiotic LHC responded: 'Has there been a mass breakout from Poitiers Jail? I've heard they keep the worst villains in there.'

He had visions of 36 prisoners - all having the surname of Mésrine - hiding in our cellar.

Dennis just laughed, saying his wife thought he was really funny - so they were both eagerly looking forward to entertaining us the next evening.

When we got to the house I, once again, had to go in first. This time I treaded more carefully than a feline Angel. There were dozens of huge frelons lying dead in the kitchen.

'*Mass suicide maybe*?' I asked myself.

None of us could work out where they had come from but they were all dead - so after about 10 minutes, the Booze Brothers decided we should go out for a Vietnamese Meal - followed by a tour of the bars.

He kept sneezing - due to hayfever - whilst I was having problems with fur balls (which I put down to the high pollen count too) but he said he would feel fine after a couple of Jenlain Ambrées and Chimays.

Mackem was equally knowledgeable about Franco-Belgians Beers, raving on about a beer made by Trappist Ducks, Duvel and Delirium Tremens. I felt that even the name of the latter had a sense of foreboding about it.

This was Mackem's first time at our maison in France. He said he needed a break after the stress of his relationship breakdown but, four days after the split, he had met a mad, blonde Geordie lass in Redcar - who was going through a divorce.

'She is great fun as she can drink like a fish and laugh (at all my jokes) like a hyena…'

I was amazed that she could understand him – he had the oddest accent I have ever heard.

He continued that she '…went like a rabbit…' I assumed he meant she was a top class sprinter, as I had heard that Gateshead was famous for producing a conveyer belt of field & track dominating talent, and: '…she is as mad as a March hare and as fit as a butcher's dog.'

I was wondering just what kind of woman he had got himself involved with. I bet David Attenborough would like to meet her. But he seemed happy enough and was looking forward to seeing her for dinner when he got home from France.

Above all, **he was looking forward to dessert…**

*'So… not only is she an Olympic-standard 400-metres sprinter, she is also a highly skilled pastry chef. Why can't my LHC meet a girl like that? Maybe he should relocate to Redcar, where the UK's most desirable women must all live.'*

I thought to myself, sadly.

Judging by the resigned look on his face, I think he was wondering the same.

After the Vietnamese meal, we embarked on a small tour of the Montmorillon bars, though I politely declined to go into Le Marchand, keeping a safe distance behind the wall outside.

They met up with some old Liverpudlian friends who had a very loud 'Essex-type' sitting with them. She had a voice like *Mary Poppins,* but it was louder than a yodelling *Tarzan*.

She looked decidedly worse for wear and the ever-friendly Liverpudlian couple seemed mightily relieved when she asked to join us - when we decided to move on. With a cat's intuition, I had a feeling this was a mistake, but could see the glint in Mackem's eye – he had clearly forgotten about his multi-animal-bodied Geordie lass.

Her booming voice seemed to get louder with every step she took up the steep hill to a superb little pub that was carved into the rock, it was called: 'La plume d'oie' and apparently was 700 years old.

As we walked in to a song about having breakfast with *The Israelis*, I thought we had somehow been transported to a bagel bar in Barbados. Everyone in the bar wore dreadlocks; a poster of Bob Marley hung behind the bar. The bar had a very unusual smell wafting around, that made me feel light-headed. They even sold Mojitos.

My LHC and I sat down at a table and he asked me what he was doing wrong, so I gave him as much sage advice as I could from a feline to a human… as he was looking more morose than a Tom that has just realised it has two little bits missing after a little trip to the vet.

Mackem, meanwhile, was doing his utmost to impress Mary Tarzan-Poppins. When a song about kayaking on the rivers in Babylon came on the jukebox, she launched herself onto the dance floor, telling Mackem how she had spent 12 hours the previous night, dancing non-stop at a music festival near Chauvigny. He was bewitched by her unique and lascivious dancing style, as if he was Herod admiring the Dance of the Seven Veils (though I don't think Herod originated from Sunderland).

A song about trying to send a message to a gentleman called Rudy came on next (amazing – a human actually not on *Facebook*) and Salomé finally decided to have a rest – much to nearly everyone's joy.

I was admiring the surroundings, when I could have sworn that, through the cannabis-induced fog, I saw a little silver tabby - who otherwise looked like me - with dreadlocks and a Rasta hat. This silver tabby was dutifully trotting along the bar carrying limes for the barman who was making the Mojitos, then it quickly disappeared - as though sensing something was not quite right.

As my LHC's bladder finally surrendered to eight Trappist Beers, he staggered off to the toilet. He left his half-full glass of Jenlain Ambrée on the table, so I thought… as he keeps raving on about it being so great, and I am 'en vacances', I'll have a little sip.

It did indeed make a pleasant change from UHT Sterilised Milk, so much so, that I finished it off.

A song about skinheads stomping around on the moon was playing, when he came back to find that

his glass was now empty. He looked at me accusingly when, to my luck, Mary Tarzan-Poppins moon-stomped over to us - until the table stopped her and she promptly asked for another Mojito… as she was flagging.

'What makes you think I drank your exceedingly pleasant Jenlain Ambrée?' I asked, nodding my head with raised eyebrows at Salomé. He just shrugged his shoulders as her eyes began to roll around and her legs began to wobble - due to the strain of dancing the Seven Veils, whilst consuming seven Mojitos... on top of a litre of Le Marchand's house wine.

'I should have been a ballet dancer with the Bolshoi... why did I have to suffer the misfortune of being born in Essex and not Moscow?' she started to wail.

Mackem came over and tried to reassure her: ' Why eye cannie lass, with them mooves you kenn always get a joob at the Black Cat Pooldunseen Club in Soonderlann. Probably betah pay than the Bolshoi anna butt the coost o' living is cheapah thun Moscoow.'

But this did not make her feel any better and Mary Poppins' voice went into Tormented Tarzan on Steroids mode:

'Maybe yaarright, ma little sugar plum fairy. Could be next best thing to the Bolshoi Ballet. Let's talk more about it where it's more intimate and less noisy **as I can't 'ear ya.** 'I'll be in the Victor Hugo tomorrow night, ma darlin', at 9 o'clock (21 hr 00) so call me on my mobile 077...'

But before she could complete her mobile number, her body, and his hopes, slumped to the floor like a dying swan.
   I had time to think: *'The whole of the Atlantic Seaboard must have heard that,'* before my head started spinning and my vision blurred. The last thing I remembered seeing was Mackem

desperately trying to revive her. Then I fell over headfirst onto an ashtray and was knocked out cold.

As I came to in a Trappist induced haze, Mackem was frenetically reading a French manual about CPR with Mary Tarzan-Poppins curled up in a ball by his feet, moaning something about being born to be a Nutcracker and being happy to change her name to Anna Kournikova if the Bolshoi would have her.

D'Artagnan was snoring loudly on a sofa, whilst a silver tabby was wrapping a bandage around my head. He kept apologising; saying something about a high-maintenance cat who wanted to marry him - but he couldn't, as he was so racked with guilt. She eventually went off with a Persian and is now living in the Haitian Embassy in Paris. They agreed to bring him along to France too and he had managed to sneak onto a TGV to Poitiers. He had been hoping for this moment, as he wanted to apologise and be good friends again.

When I realised it was a truly contrite Winston, with his head bowed, we stood up and shook paws - as I addressed the woolly Rasta hat:

'It does no-one any good to go through life bearing grudges and a real cat should be man enough (metaphorically at least) to accept a sincere apology, especially when family or close friends are concerned.'

On that philosophical note, I promptly fell off the table and knocked myself out again.

Luckily for the Three Musketeers, Dennis was not picking us up until 14:00 hrs the next day - to take us to Le Bal-Trap at Poitiers.

The place was packed with off-season hunters, honing their musketry skills on what looked like various bits of orange crockery flying through the air - presumably they were seconds from the porcelain factories in Limoges. I half-expected an irate, vodka-fuelled, chain-smoking social worker to come bursting out of a copse of trees, armed with a dinner set - but that never happened.

Dennis briefed us on what we had to do and I was given the task of pressing a button with my paw. As soon as the shooter said 'Tirer' – paw on button would release an orange disc. Seemed easy enough to me.

Dennis briefed Wyatt Earp and Doc Halliday on how to handle the 'up & under' shotgun: holding it tight into the shoulder and looking upwards at all times. He said that they had to aim in front of the dinner plate as it flew through the air and follow through - after gently squeezing the trigger.

'Dead easy. Just relax, breathe gently and **let the shotgun do the work**...'

*'What could possibly go wrong?'* I thought to myself.

They were given twenty-five cartridges each and were to take it in turn. Whoever lost had to buy everyone a drink in the bar afterwards, though looking at the state of the Trappist Comancheros, another beer was the last thing they needed.

The Mackem gunslinger went first.

Dennis was showing him how to caress the weapon. *'He's the last person you should be saying that to,'* I thought when a shout of **TIRER** boomed through the woods. Being aware of what had been described as: '…having the most responsible task of all four of us - as a shotgun at short range is lethal…' I instantly pressed down with my paw.

A dinner plate went flying through the air but dopey Mackem was still learning how to *caress* his weapon.

'0 out of 1,' announced the adjudicator.
'But I wasn't ready…' bemoaned the gunslinger, whilst Wyatt looked at me with a conspiratorial smirk on his face. Mackem continued to protest…

'…I didn't say TIRER. Someone ov…'

Like one of Pavlov's more obedient dogs, I pressed down on the other button…

'0 out of 2. Change over.'

Wyatt took up his position, leaning so far forward I thought he was doing an impression of a Springer Spaniel.
I was unable to resist temptation, so shouted: 'Fetch' but he didn't move.

Then I was told:
'Ssshhh. No Talking.'

'Sorry…'

'Ssssssshhhhhhh.'

After a pause of what seemed like 15 minutes… *'Has he gone to sleep standing up?'* It was like a stand off from a Spaghetti Western, but he finally whispered:

'Sorry, Dennis, I forgot. What am I supposed to shout?'

'Aahh, for God's sake… **TIRER.**'

Button instantly pressed with the reflexes of a Pavlovian Mongoose.
'0 out of 1'.

Muttering something about that 'disloyal bloody cat' he resumed his somewhat ridiculous *firing / sleeping / springer spaniel sniffing* stance - which I did find amusing and let out a small snigger just after he said TIRER, whilst still being - I am very impressed to say - in auto-paw button pressing mode. Unfortunately, he had turned around to tell me to stop distracting him - when the dinner plate went shooting past him… towards the moon.

'0 out of 2. Change over. Did you say you both spent time in the TA? Not the Infantry, I hope?'

On only his 11th attempt, El Pistolero Mackem obliterated a plate to take a 1-0 lead - which he maintained, until Wyatt had his final 2 shots.

'Okay, Rick, Mackem is winning 3-2. You've now got the opportunity to win with your final two rounds.'

At which point, El Pistolero started crooning in a Sunderland-cum-Wyoming cowboy accent, the famous ballad from High Noon… –

Dennis offered some helpful advice: 'Just keep looking along the barrel. Then, when you see the disc, just follow it and fire in front of it.'

As soon as he shouted TIRER, the pollen count hit him and he sneezed violently, causing the shotgun to fire to the left, just missing an adjoining group of three French bal-trappers - showering them with shrapnel comprised of pine needles (from the pellet-splattered branches immediately above their heads).

I wasn't quite sure what they shouted as we were all wearing ear protectors, but I don't think it was along the lines of: '…gently caress your weapon'.

After running over to apologise to the nearly decapitated tirailleurs, which included promising to buy each of them a bottle of Scotch as an apology, he doubled back through the bushes like a character from *The Last of the Mohicans*.

'How about we let Nelson have a go, if he promises not to shoot anyone?'

Although I was keen, my front legs weren't long enough, so I was back to detonating duties. It was then decided that whoever lost, had to buy the three bottles of Scotch for the Huron War Party in the adjoining bushes.

Looking like Cora Munro's life rested on this last cartridge, he assumed his previous stance, then I suddenly felt a fur ball get lodged in my throat. I couldn't breathe.

'TIRER.'

I was doubled up wheezing, so didn't hear his command.

**'TIRER!'**

By this time, I had great trouble breathing and was trying to cough up the fur ball - whilst not daring to let go of the detonator.

**'TIIIIIRRRREEEEER!!!!'**

It was such a blood-curdling scream that Mackem and Dennis jumped into the nearest bush for fear of being scalped by Magua and his band of renegade braves. I dropped the detonator and ran up the nearest pine tree, hoping that even if all of the Huron Braves stood on top of each other - as a human ladder - they would still be unable to reach me at the top of the tree.

At the same time, 26 clays went flying through the sky, leading to a nervous breakdown of a flock of geese that had foolishly decided to fly overhead. The huge leader of the geese, flying at the front of the delta shape, was mortally wounded by 5 clay discs and 3 shotgun cartridges (*serves him right for showboating,* I thought).

Its dying dive down to earth fell 6ft short as it landed on top of Wyatt's head, knocking him out instantly.

Magua and his braves seemed to come running from all directions, so I decided it was best to stay where I was, near the top of the pine tree, until I noticed they were all slapping Chingachgook and Uncas on the back, offering them sips from their brandy flasks, congratulating and thanking them for the big goose, which they would put on the post-shoot barbecue.

*'No wonder the Iroquois were defeated so easily.'* I mused.

They all forget about Hawkeye, presumably as he was entirely covered in goose feathers.

'If nothing else, he will be well-insulated,' I thought, as I gingerly inched my way down the tree and quietly past his prone body - conscious that he still had one cartridge with which to shoot me - and at least they hadn't scalped him. So, I joined the others for the barbecue and a well-deserved saucer of milk. To my amazement, I was the toast of the pow-wow and was made an Honorary Member.

The three survivors agreed that it had been a most enjoyable afternoon.

After two days in Poitiers Hospital, the noble Mohican warrior 'Man With Flattened Head' was let out in time to take Mackem to Le Pont du chêne for a farewell Grimbergen, prior to Dennis driving him to the airport. After telling everyone he couldn't wait to see his Geordie lass again - having forgotten about Mary Tarzan-Poppins in the time it takes to shout 'Ungawa' - we got up to leave, then he popped to the toilet '…for a minute.'

So we waited by the entrance.

After fifteen minutes of waiting for Godot, my LHC tried to converse with the very nice French Lady who owned the bar.

'J'ai repris le sport du bal-trap, Madame.'
*'I have taken up the sport of clay pigeon shooting, Madam.'*

'Ah, très bon Monsieur. C'est un magnifique sport français. Vous l'aimez ?'
*'Ah, very good Sir. It is a magnificent French sport. Do you like it ?'*

'Bien sûr mais c'est très dangereux.'
*'Certainly but it is very dangerous.'*

'Ouuuuuiiiii ?' ('*Reeeaalllly*?') she said with arched eyebrows and an elongated tone, expressing wonderment.

At this point, Dennis, even though he came from Nottingham, started to speak in fluent French to the other patrons, hoping they would think he was **not** the mad Rosbif's mate. I decided to sit under a table at the far end of the bar.

'Parce que j'ai été presque tué par une énorme oie volante.'
*'Because I was almost killed by an enormous flying goose.'*

At which point the rest of the bar turned around to listen to: 'cette histoire incroyable du rosbif fou.'

'L'oie a-t-elle mis le feu de retour à vous avec un fusil de chasse?' she asked, with a smile as wide as the Seine
*'Did the goose fire back at you with a shotgun?'*

The five Frenchmen at the bar, all looked at each other and started doing that annoying Gallic shrug, but were doing it non-stop like beret-topped piston engines.

*'Probably the most active they've been for the past 35 years,'* I thought disdainfully, having noted that rush hour in France (Tuesday to Thursday only) is onze heures cinquante and treize heures cinquante-cinq.

Having never heard that wisest of expressions: '…when you are in a hole, stop digging', Man With Flattened Head or L'homme avec la tête aplatie, continued his remarkable tale:
'Non, elle est tombée du ciel et a débarqué sur ma tête.'
*'No, it fell from the sky and landed on my head.'*

'Ooh la la. Ce doit avoir été une oie de bombardier de stuka.'
*'Stone the crows. It must have been a Stuka Bomber goose.'*

This resulted in uproarious laughter in the bar.
One old French lady commented that had she known 30 years ago that there was a regular stand-up comedy routine, she would have come more often. She then asked Marcel Marceau if she could have his autograph, which made him even more crimson-featured - as the old men at the bar started clapping and shouting: 'Bravo' and 'Encore'.
With perfect comic timing, his sidekick emerged from the toilet… after 55 minutes.

'What on earth have you been doing for the past hour? Did you get stuck?'

'No, I had just finished on the crapper (human litter tray) when Sadie called me to say it was all over. I'm gutted. She could have been the one...' he lamented, with the pathos of a true comedy great.

*'Hang on a minute…'* I thought. *'It was comatose Salomé three nights ago...'*

A sad Mackem flew back to the UK, no doubt regretting buying Mary Tarzan-Poppins one Mojito too many (at €9.50 each) and normal life resumed.

My LHC invited his French neighbours round for a meal that night, which was very nice, although they expressed wide-eyed amazement that he should give me some Bayonne Ham and Camembert, as they just fed their cats scraps: not even dry cat food. Perhaps living in England isn't so bad after all.

I decided never to touch his Jenlain Ambrée ever again and had a much more mellow night's sleep - until I awoke with an itching sensation on the end of my nose at 4:00 a.m.

There was a huge black and yellow hornet staring back at me with a fearsome Vincent Cassel-esque grimace - as though I had murdered its entire family.

We had been told for the umpteenth time last night, but this time by our French neighbours, so we now stopped laughing about it, that a single hornet could kill a cat or a human with just one sting.

I was so shocked that I shot off the recently

vacated Lyons iron bed, and shook my head, then looked all around me with a soupçon of blind panic. But, thankfully, it was nowhere to be seen.

So I sat back down purring with relief that the hornet had disappeared and wondering what all the fuss was about. I started to drift off back to sleep; contentedly dreaming about Fanny. Thirteen seconds later I suffered the most agonising pain in my buttocks that I have ever experienced in my entire life. I shot upwards and only halted when I hit the ceiling fan (la plafonnière).

I came back down rolling in agony on the bed and it buzzed off out of the window.

**'Aaaarrrggghhh. I've been attacked by a FRELON...'** I screamed in agony.

The intrepid warrior (Man With Flattened Head) came bounding in, armed with, of all things, a Swiss Army Knife.

'Quick. Hide in the cupboard. I'll call the Gendarmes. Thank God it's not Sunday. Their unité de réponse rapide (Rapid Response Unit) will be here by no later than seize heures trente. How many convicts were there? Maybe if I call Dennis he'll come straight over with his shotgun. Holy Merde. Were any called Mésrine or did they look like Vincent Cassel? We'll really be knackered then.'

Being knackered was the least of my worries, at this particular point in time:

'It was a **HORNET!!!** You demented rosbif. Aaaarrrggghhhh... '

I continued to yodel in agony. I had not been in this much pain since I tried eating five pieces of his *Toblerone* bar all in one go.

Then tranquillity suddenly descended upon Jim Bowie:
'A wasp...? Is that all??? A harmless, little wasp???' Enquired Dr Dolittle empathically, before going back to his room to sleep off a bottle of Cote du Rhône.

I continued to scream and roll around in agony, having not had such a burning sensation in my buttocks since the day after I was treated to a Lamb Madras on my birthday - the previous year.

He got up four hours later, complaining that he couldn't bear to listen to my *'pathetic screaming'* any longer, which I have to say did not make me feel like the most valued cat in the house. He eventually managed to find a Vet that was open in Chauvigny.

Upon entering the Vet's Maison de douleur in my *Harp Air* cat-carrying tumbril, empathising with how Danton must have felt on the way to his rendezvous with Madame Guillotine, my day actually succeeded in taking a turn for the worse.

It started off very well as Chauvigny's veterinary answer to Emmanuelle Béart, Dr. Marie-Madeleine Boucher, glided serenely into the room and took me out of my carrier. The pain had by this time subsided to the point that I had stopped screaming - but I had a massive, red sore where the frelon had stung me.

Dr. Boucher gently inspected my gaping wound then, in perfect English, told Dolittle that it was indeed so nasty that it could turn the surrounding area gangrenous - so one option to avoid the risk of septicaemia was:

…NEUTERING ☠ ☠

Just as Dr. Boucher was saying this, a bespectacled Junior Vet edged his smiling face to mine and tried to fool me into relaxing, prior to putting me into a half-Nelson, then strapping me down on the operating/amputating table, by saying:
'Ah, quel chat gentil. Nelson est vraiment un nom charmant. Comment vas-tu mon petit amiral?'

But he under-estimated my intelligence, probably thinking I was as stupid as my still-bandaged human companion. I wasn't going to be foxed by his 'faux charme'.

Luckily, the BBC's recent 'Big Cat Diary' was my favourite documentary and was effectively a training manual *par excellence* for extreme events such as this.

Remembering how leopards did it, I launched myself at the assistant cat castrator, grabbing him by the throat with both front paws and hanging on for dear life as he started whirling round like a screaming Dervish:

**'Au secours. Ce chat est un assassin!!'**

We seemed to be going in circles so fast that I thought I would end up using him to drill an escape route through the linoleum floor.

My LHC apologetically stepped forward to intervene, but he was sent sprawling over the operating table as my rear legs effectively gave him a double roundhouse kick to the jaw - unintentionally knocking him out. By this point, the Junior Vet - who was now regretting not studying Law at L'Université de Lyon (in accordance with his father's wishes) – slumped to the floor semi-conscious. I then let go of him and was totally exhausted - both mentally and physically. I decided that if I was to be a leopard, I would have to either be a vegetarian or live next to a supermarket.

The good news was that the pain in my buttocks had gone away.

As my LHC groggily rose to his feet and the Junior Vet attempted to hide in my cat carrier, I stood and waited - as stoically as Hector awaiting the final, mortal onslaught from Achilles.

Dr. Boucher then turned to my LHC, who was by now crying out for the fair green fields of England and his cat-free sanctuary of an office where he would never again complain of having to work 60-hour weeks.

*'Poor devil, must be hallucinating again,'* I thought, showing more empathy for him in that instant than he had done all morning for my own plight.

Dr. Boucher said, in still perfect English:

'However the much better alternative, which I was going to recommend before I was rudely interrupted, is a course of antibiotics and some antiseptic cream.'

My LHC and I both stared at her, then at each other, then looked up at the stars and collapsed...

The next day, Monsieur Assassin des Frelons, who I presumed - judging by his outfit - was also in training to be a deep sea diver, came out to fumigate the house. This fumigation resulted in the deaths of dozens of frelons; which gave us inordinate satisfaction, relief and joy.

The rest of the holiday was comparatively mundane, though he became obsessed with counting down the hours to the time the plane departed from Limoges.

On the day we finally were to leave, he got a letter from the Vet which was a nice touch, probably asking if I had made a full recovery as I had heard the French medical system was second to none and prided itself on its superlative patient care.

My LHC, who had so many bandages wrapped around his head that he looked like the Invisible Man en vacances, had decided it was safest for him to stay in bed as long as possible until checking in at Limoges Airport, so I gingerly sat down by my milk saucer and half-eaten croissant and opened her letter:

Cher Monsieur Vaughan,

Please find attached our bill for Sunday's emergency veterinary appointment:

Call out fee - €75
Antibiotics - €44

Antiseptic cream - €21
*New for old* replacement operating table - €100
Dr. Renard's medical treatment for injuries
inflicted by your cat - €350
Psychological counselling for Dr Renard (6 x 1
hour sessions) - €480
Total Bill - €1,070
TVA at 20% - €214

**GRAND TOTAL =        €1,284**

We do hope your cat has made a full recovery – regrettably the same cannot be said of my highly traumatised colleague, Dr Renard, who is presently on indefinite sick leave. I have managed to dissuade him from pressing criminal charges against you - on condition that neither you nor your cat ever visit our surgery again.

Cordialement,
Dr. M-M. Boucher


I thought this seemed exceptionally good value in the circumstances.

The flight back to the UK passed without incident and I even got upgraded to a seat in Cattle Class. He was very subdued however, presumably upset about having to return to work.

But I had had a great time and couldn't wait to return later in the summer.

# July

**Allez Allez Allez Monsieur Wiggo!!!**

July proved to be a quiet month as my LHC recovered from his injuries. The highlight of the month was Le Tour de France, inspiring him even further to 'get on the bloody bike' in France in August.

'I'm fed up renovating the house and am looking forward to getting on a road bike and having an invigorating and relaxing holiday, touring rural France. This is why I bought the house and it will be much more fun than sailing around the Caribbean with a crew of drunkards.'

That infamous holiday in the Caribbean, which was like being marooned on a tiny boat with a toxic cross between the Ku Klux Klan and relapsed alcoholics suffering from collective amnesia when it came to paying their bar bills each day, sparked unpleasant memories for me too and I agreed that touring around on deserted roads - where there was no risk of being run over by a car or lorry - had much to recommend it.

In fact, the biggest danger we could think of was coming across a snake or running over a myopic pheasant. Roll on August, we concurred.

My LHC spends every night staring and shouting at his own reflection in the TV screen (and he thinks cats are stupid), much to my annoyance, as I try to concentrate on watching Le Tour de France. I even gave up chasing rodents. Amazingly, it was the first time an Englishman, albeit one born in Ghent and with an Antipodean sire, won Le Tour. He is definitely one cool cat, although I did feel he could have exercised a little more sangfroid during the press conference when his language was more colourful than *'son maillot jaune'.*

Who would have thought a Rosbif would win the Tour de France? There again, who would have thought the French President would be called Holland(e) or that the French don't have a word for 'entrepreneur'?

I could, however, understand the modish wearer of *le maillot jaune* being annoyed by the snide and asinine questions re: doping. Perhaps they could not handle the fact that a rosbif was winning the TDF? Or perhaps he was being quizzed by an undercover Texan Journalist? If it had been me I would have insouciantly replied:

*Of course we are **ALL** drugged up to the eyeballs, you imbeciles, how else do you expect us to cycle up and down the Alps, Mont Ventoux and then the Pyrenees? By the way, has anyone seen a branch of Boots the Chemist in the Limousin? All these ridiculous questions are giving me a headache.'*

It made me proud to be a British Blue when he mounted the winner's podium in Paris. I wish that I could have been seated next to him with Fanny (she could have sat next to Tommy Voeckler) but her FCH had taken her en vacances to Les Antilles. I must admit that I thought Les Antilles was a character from *Coronation Street* or *Neighbours,* hence once more illuminating the gulf in class between us.

I got quite emotional when Wiggo mounted the winner's podium, though he was as cool as a mod with an open cheque book in a *Vespa* Dealership.

Then an opera singer joined the joyous proceedings wearing a dress that could not have been more patriotic had the Queen designed it. That made me even more emotional and I sneezed violently over the pet Yorkshire Terrier of a Parisienne bystander. Its gratuitous response was to stare up at me with slowly widening eyes, bare its teeth and growl at me. I thought it was very brave of her to sing *'God Save The Queen'* at the conclusion of France's most famous and prestigious sporting event, especially as the ratio of Rosbifs to Frenchmen was even less favourable than that at Agincourt - and the Parisians were still smarting at a vélo-rosbif winning the Tour de France for the first time in its entire history.

Clearly adapting Henry V's rallying speech, viz. *'Cry God for Wiggo, England and Team Sky'* and heartily embracing his spirit of *'Once more unto the breach dear friends, once more...'* she launched into the national anthem to the unadulterated chagrin of 200,000 disgruntled Parisians.

Whilst keeping one eye on the belligerent Yorkshire Terrier, whose tiresome growling was becoming so loud it was starting to drown out the singing, I furtively looked around me and noticed that the British national anthem was beginning to *'...stiffen the sinews and summon up the blood'* of the local populace (plus one dog). As she got to the second verse, a Gitane-smoking sexagenarian

Frenchman standing to my right grumbled with indignation, becoming of the ancien regime, that not even Robespierre had caused so much harm to a Monarch: clearly a loyal supporter of the House of Bourbon, I summised. But I thought her singing was very good bearing in mind she did not have any supporting musicians. I put this down to the Massed Bands of the Guards Division having presumably been made redundant under yet more government cuts. Personally, I would have preferred the Massed Pipes of the Black Watch, the Gordon Highlanders, the King's Own Scottish Borderers and the Royal Highland Fusiliers - but I expect these fine old regiments no longer exist either.

I suppose we should just be thankful this Government was not in power in 1805 otherwise we would be listening *to: Les cornemuses et tambours du deuxième bataillon des Fusiliers Highland de l'Empereur.*

It also made me realise it was such a shame that the modern racing bike no longer comes equipped with a horn as the rest of Team Sky could have then provided a brass section if nothing else.

Another Frenchman standing to my left swore he heard the by now distressed-looking Wiggo mumbling something about wishing he had represented his country of birth as the Parisians would not have objected to Plastic Bertrand singing 'La Brabançonne'. But I think Wiggo's pained expression was due to him getting as worried as I was that we would be lynched by the infamous Parisian mob, due to the temerity of a handful of Rosbifs making 200,000 Frenchmen stand to attention, whilst the plucky diva finished off her marvellous rendition of *'God save the Queen'*.

Perhaps if she had sung a *'Whole lot of rosbifs'* that may have been a bit less galling for the Gallic members of the audience. Like a greyhound in the slips, I was ready to make a dash for it, but the crowd finally let up a huge cheer when it was announced that their compatriot Thomas Voeckler had won the coveted award of King of the Mountains. So, I could finally relax in the knowledge that all's well that ends well.

## August

**Death on Le Col de Pindray**

We went to France for the month. Nice holiday, but it meant that I was unable to be the mascot for Team GB. I did manage to watch the opening ceremony and I hadn't before realised that the Queen was a paratrooper. Next thing you know she will be competing in the Tour de France. A wonderful lady and an inspiration to us all, especially pensioners.

I was suitably unimpressed by the yahooing and whooping Team USA. Couldn't they just march with a modicum of humility and decorum behind the Stars and Stripes… like the tiny pacific nation of Nauru?

I believe that Nauru, like many pacific islands, used to be inhabited by fearsome cannibals. The only member of Team Nauru looked so big and fearsome that I reckon he could have carried the plane to Heathrow. I just hope that Team USA never enlist in the Coldstream Guards otherwise the Trooping of the Colour will never be the same again as, in between yahooing and whooping all the way down Pall Mall, they continually ask members of the public to look after their rifles whilst they take photos of each other on their mobile phones

I was even more unimpressed when the Welsh members of the Team GB Soccer Team refused to sing the national anthem. What were they expecting: Tom Jones belting out Delilah? I bet David Beckham would have sung his heart out. I was most perplexed that they did not allow him to play, after all he had done to bring the Olympics to London.

Inspired no doubt by a certain person's heroics, my idiotic LHC decided to go cycling every day on his brand new *Bianchi* road bike... in the middle of a heat wave in France. The Gendarmes were pleading with everyone to do nothing, stay indoors, keep cool and drink lots of water.

He actually expected me to go out with him on his 50km rides and I cordially reminded him that: only mad dogs and Englishmen (please note zero reference to the clearly more intelligent cats) go out in the midday sun. Then I sat in the shade all day with a bowl of *Perrier*, some Camembert wrapped in Bayonne Ham (Fanny would have been impressed) and my favourite Dostoyevsky novel.

I think the real reason he wanted me to run along next to him was so that he could send me off for help if he had a puncture (as though I would know where to go - I am a feline… not a homing pigeon). The fool should have bought himself a cheetah or a mechanically-minded St Bernard.

The next day, whilst in Poitiers, he thought that it would be a grand idea to buy himself a pair of leather Moroccan slippers and asked me if I thought he looked cool and sophisticated in them.

Absolutely… so much so that I told him it was a shame he had not treated himself to a Fez too - as I am sure they will be all the rage in the Giro d'Italia.

Then, in a supreme act of sartorially self-indulgent stupidity, he bought himself a matching *Bianchi* winter cycling jersey for €145 - on the day the temperature outside le Magasin Vélo-Sport hit 45 degrees in the shade. I suggested that he ask the shop if they sold Ushankas too. So he did.

With a visage of incredulity, the owner said he would have to wait until *Bianchi*'s winter catalogue came out.

We did manage to watch one, very unusual, Olympic event called the *Kierin*. Never heard of it before. It was so dangerous that it had its own funeral director, though I felt he should have been following the riders - not the other way round. Shame Wiggo wasn't competing, as I am sure he would have had a word with the organisers and asked them to replace the Funeral Director's moped with something more stylish: a *Suzuki Burgman 200* would have fitted the bill.

My deluded LHC wants to give the Kierin a go when we return to the UK. I may as well take his body measurements now and order a coffin…

We were very disappointed that Cav didn't win a medal and, to add salt to his wounds, some cycling vampire from Kazakhstan won the Gold – he had previously been banned from cycling for blood doping. No wonder he looked so pale.

My LHC had decided that the spirit of Wiggo, if not Tommy Simpson, had been instilled in him and he was to complete his own - self-styled - Tour de Vienne. I pointed out to him that La Vienne is not exactly renowned for its mountain peaks, unless he counted the hill leading up to Pindray. His not being 'un Chasseur des Cols' was probably revealed by his utter failure to buy cycling kit - unless his *Vespa* Scooter mug and Crédit Agricole water bottle counted.

So, in the amount of time it takes Ricardo Ciclismo-Caballero to take 12 types of performance-enhancing barbiturates and cycle up Mont Ventoux and back down again… then flatly deny ever having indulged in a *paracetamol* in his entire life - (his Minnie Mouse voice may, however, raise suspicions amongst Les Gendarmes du Doping) - he bought so much cycling kit from *Wiggle* that he became a Gold Customer in less time than you can say 'anabolic steroids'.

'Formidable, non?' He asked me rhetorically with his Voltaire-esque command of French.

'How much gourmet cat food could you have bought me instead?' I asked poignantly, before telling him how impressed I was with his command of the French Language after 3.5 years at night school.

I was surprised that he was not made an Honorary Member of *Team Wiggle*; though they did not enter a team in 2012. Perhaps they were worried he would be at grave risk of being banned for drug taking, due to the fact that he has about 12 mugs of coffee each day.

On his second trip, also during the heat wave, I was persuaded (*threatened* by the thought of a six-month diet of dry cat food and sterilised long life milk), to come along on his ride to Saint Savin.

He must have been reading one of those stupid American Books on motivation and self-actualisation such as: 'If I can become a millionaire in 4 years by selling ceiling fans to the Inuit, then so can **you**…' as he told me that we were a team and that there is no 'i' in team.

I curtly pointed out that there is indeed an 'i' in the French word for team, and that being based in France à ce moment he should buy himself a French Dictionary along with a book on basic bike maintenance.

For this supposed act of insolence, Le Roi du Tour de Vienne, if not Le Président de l'équipe, told me I would be sleeping in the cellar for the rest of the holiday and would have to take my chances with the serpents each night.

As a final act of defiance, I mentioned that if these serpents were actually *vipeurs* then at least I would not be alone. But this parting shot of irony was lost on him.

So, after spending 45 minutes trying to click his new Shimano cycling shoes into the pedals, we finally set off past the charming little hamlet of

Pruniers and then onto Pindray. We stopped momentarily to look at the charred remains of the château then in a Banzai moment of daring/stupidity he decided to go hell for leather down the hill leading from Pindray to Jouhet... I was hanging on for dear life to the handlebars with all 4 legs, whilst trying to press one brake lever with my tail, as he hurtled downwards at 98 km per hour.

He did cut an incongruous figure on his beautiful *Bianchi*, not just on account of his abject incompetence and the crazed grin on his face (which might have been due to the wind), but also because he was dressed in his non-Lycra, paint splattered cargo shorts, bright orange *Heineken* Baseball Cap and *Ajax Amsterdam* T-Shirt (he wasn't prepared to wait 48 hours for his delivery from *Wiggle*).

At least he did have a proper pair of cycling shoes with *cleats* or *'******* stupid ******* cleats'* as he called them, whilst trying to mount his Bianchi - which I thought was a most distinctive brand name.

We went past a very nice little café-bar-cum-restaurant at Jouhet called 'Le Col de Gartempe' (which I did think was a bit of an odd name) where I leapt off and kissed the ground with papal sincerity, whilst he proudly marched into the bar and ordered a Pastis 'just one for the road' he said with a glint in his *Oakley*-covered eyes.

I hobbled in with a limp, in the hope that someone would intervene and tell Tommy Simpson II, who was muttering to the Pastis Peloton about me displaying a contemptible lack of sangfroid, that I was in no fit state to 'get back on the bloody bike.'

The kind and friendly bar owners mistook me for a Chartreux and instantly adopted me as the team mascot for both their darts team and local rugby club. This resulted in a saucer of fresh goat's milk plus a dish of saumon fumé - which I found very agreeable. Now this is my kind of bar.

Unfortunately, the 'Le Col de Gartempe' Darts Team, including a gorgeous younger version of Brigitte Bardot (the 2nd reason for this being my kind of bar), was having a practise session so, ninety minutes later, and with Pastis-induced boldness, he decided it was time to head back to Pindray to tackle his first Col (which begged the question of: why didn't we just stay where we were in the first place?).

After struggling up to the summit of Le Col de Pindray (which I suggested, without a soupçon of sarcasm, should be named L'assassin de buveurs de pastis) in an unorthodox zigzag manner and in totally the wrong gear (ou Le Col des bouffons, peut-être), he stopped to admire his epic achievement and shouted *'Je suis sans doute le roi des...'* then was promptly flattened by a massive 180 kilo wild boar, that flew out of nowhere just outside what remains of the Château at Pindray.

This was the closest I had ever seen to a flying pig... other than an ex-Rangers keeper.

With its dying breath, the sanglier gored him in his thigh with its tusks, and he lay there screaming in agony, with blood pouring out of his leg... like water gushing out of a burst mains pipe - his beautiful *Bianchi* totally shredded.

Luckily, I managed to leap clear and, being a cat, I landed on my paws in a field full of sunflowers.

Having not been trained in First Aid, and being a bit squeamish at the sight of blood, I decided to go pheasant chasing in an adjoining field for a couple of hours.

Then I felt guilty (and exhausted) so came back and sat next to my LHC - in a magnanimous attempt to keep his spirits up by telling him that the sanglier was now deceased - so we potentially had a year's supply of Bayonne Ham.

At least he wasn't wearing his brand new €145 *Bianchi* Winter Cycling Jersey... which would have been totally ruined. For some reason, this didn't perk him up and he lay there groaning and generally rambling on incoherently about his bronze level travel insurance **not** including free ambulance cover - which I put down to Pastis-induced delirium.

I don't think I helped matters by suggesting he might have been better off investing in a set of darts.

As he lay there groaning in agony he begged: 'Nelson, please could you sprint back to our house my loyal, little chum and check my travel insurance policy - otherwise I fear I may have to bid you farewell forever unless a kindly Transylvanian cyclist from Team Vlad passes by and offers to give me an entire blood transfusion.'

I had to sit down and think about this as I was quite exhausted. I had been chasing the pheasants in 45 degrees Celsius heat for the past 2 hours - but he did look more dead than alive so, holding the house keys in my mouth, I trotted off through the lane then, once out of sight, slowed down to a walking pace on a par with the march of the French Foreign Legion.

After taking a cat nap for about 2 hours, I dug out all of his holiday documents and opened up the envelope that contained the travel insurance paperwork. Bronze was indeed the cheapest level of cover available. I noticed that the parsimonious old miser had only bothered to include himself on his travel insurance cover, but I was more concerned at the prospect of having to drag him to Montmorillon Hospital… I was supposed to be on holiday.

I was putting all of the papers together in a neat pile when I found a separate letter in an envelope on which he had scribbled:

**'Highly Confidential: DO NOT SHOW CAT'** from Sauve Qui Peut Insurance Ltd.

What could this be? His will perhaps? And there I was, complaining about having to drag him eight kilometres to hospital. I suppose I should have been ashamed of myself, although that sentiment is an alien concept to felines.

Deciding that I would die of curiosity if the contents were not revealed, I first filled up a water bottle and put that next to his book of French Medical Expressions to take back to him then, feeling guilty, I opened the letter.

*'Perhaps he has nominated that all of his assets are to go to me in the event of his untimely death or permanent incapacity,'* I thought, with a heavy heart. *'He's not*

*such a bad chap really*,' I mused, with a rare pang of affection.

Then I reminisced about all of the good times we'd had: watching *Match of the Day;* listening to *Gun n' Roses* whilst beating him at chess; watching him clean out my litter tray; ripping up his corduroy trousers along the custom-made tramlines; touring the French countryside; hanging out in Le Paradis des Trappistes and even persuading him to go to church on Sundays, when in France.

Perhaps I had been harsh on my loyal human companion, so with glazed eyes and a warm glow in the cockles of my heart I started to read its contents:


'Dear Mr Vaughan,

Thank you for your recent letter and please accept this response as our acknowledgement.

We are very sorry to hear that you have decided to cancel your pet insurance cover as you firmly believe you have far better things to spend your hard-earned money on.

We acknowledge that we have previously written to you six times on this matter over the past four months, so please accept our heartfelt apologies for what you described as 'futile harassment'.

We realise that we have failed to convince you of the merits of insuring your beloved companion, even though you said in each previous rejection of our increasingly discounted offers that, even on the pain of death, these are the last two words you would ever use to describe 'that damned cat'.

You told us in your 6th letter rejecting our latest offer (we are very sorry but we really cannot offer you a 95% discount plus 12 months supply of *Cat Master Chef* Duck à l'Orange) that, '…even if cats ruled the world, I still would not insure Nelson.'

All of the girls in the Contact Centre think that Nelson is such a gorgeous name and feel that your little feline companion - a handsome British Blue to boot - must be absolutely adorable and not really 'obnoxious and insolent in equal measure' as you insist.

So please let us have this final opportunity (as we respect your threat to sue us and complain to Which Magazine) to respectfully assure you that:

1. Insuring Nelson is not a complete waste of money.

2. Cat food, cat litter and vet's bills are not other worthless drains on your finances.

3. Animals, especially cats, are worthy creatures deserving of our unconditional love; and

4. 99.8% of our policyholders hold their pets in the highest esteem: regarding them as integral, important and much-loved members of the family.

5. We feel compelled to refute your arguments that:

a. these 99.8% of policyholders are 'clearly psychotic imbeciles'; or that

b. you are in the 0.2% who regard their pet cats as an 'unappreciative, malevolent and blood-sucking blight on their lives'.

Please note we did not find either of these verbatim comments in our research of 2,500 policyholders.

We did, however, like your amusing aside about holding your garden gnomes in higher esteem than Nelson as 'at least they don't answer me back…'

Despite my phlegmatic British Heritage, I was a bit upset and whatever sympathy I had for him drained out of me as quickly as the contents of Toulouse Lautrec's hollow walking cane.

I no longer felt compelled to rush back, so decided to wander back via 'Le Col de Gartempe' before heading off to admire the skewered Tommy Simpson and nonchalantly enquire as to whether the Marketing Director of Sauve Qui Peut (Pet Insurance Division) and all of the girls in the Contact Centre, may care to hear my side of the story.

But, by the time I had reached him, his mind had gone - poor devil.

I watched him babbling along incoherently, thinking:

*'If he was a horse, and I a vet, I would shoot him… with inordinate pleasure, starting with his kneecaps.'*

But only after checking whether gunshot wounds were covered by his Bronze Level insurance.

Six hours had elapsed since his apocalyptic encounter with the four legs of Bayonne Ham. It was Dimanche in rural France and the sun was starting to set. Then, when a van full of Gendarmes finally came zooming along and screeched to a halt, they ran over his other leg which was already impaled on 4 spokes of the rear wheel.

Closest he's ever come to acupuncture.

Instead of taking him to hospital they arrested him on suspicion of having stolen the bike. For which he got 15 days in Poitiers Jail plus an extra 31 days for cruelty to an animal - plus a bonus 7 days for hunting without a licence. So... I trotted home, thinking I could trade up that night, from sleeping with a nest of vipers to napping in his double-sized bed: C'était sans doute un bon résultat.

After three weeks, I decided to pay him a visit. He was finally able to hobble around his 9' by 6' prison cell unaided and he actually seemed genuinely pleased to see me, especially when he saw the huge package which I had brought for him, compliments of Chez *Wiggle*. He really perked up as he strutted around on one leg in his pink lycra cycling shorts, until we both looked out of his prison cell window to see Le Commandant des Gendarmes whizzing past shouting 'Allez Allez Allez' on his beautifully restored *Bianchi* bike and - to add insult to injury - he was wearing his *Heineken* Cap.

So... having now spent more money at *Wiggle* in a week than British Politicians claim in expenses in a year, he was the sportiest looking inmate in Poitiers Jail. Meanwhile, I was enjoying a bonus holiday in the heat wave.

# September

**Lost in translation**

1st: Dumped by Fanny.

I felt as if I had been transported to an island of complete and utter emotional desolation (the leper-infested L'île du Diable with just Les for company) – and it was all due to a simple, linguistic misunderstanding.

Please allow me to put this in context: each night for dinner during August she would be late, spending hours in the bathroom brushing her fur, putting gel on her whiskers and painting her claws.

After the 21st successive night, all I said was:

'Please stop fannying around, otherwise we'll be late yet again for dinner and miss both the lobster bisqué and boeuf bourguignon.'

Well, mea culpa, I unleashed the full fury of the hounds of hell when I gently purred those irrevocable words. She went more ballistic than a Mayan Shaman who had been given a 2013 calendar for Xmas.

My military comparisons were instantly demoted and I now understood how Capitaine Dreyfuss must have felt at his unjust trial. Malheureusement, Émile Zola was not on hand to lend his support, having been dead for 110 years.

I tried to make amends by offering her my bottle of flea drops topped up with absinthe - but that only made matters worse.

**Hell hath no fury like a feline besmirched.**

She cordially informed me that she has never had fleas… **EVER -** and after 40 minutes (the time it takes Stade Toulousain to put 30 unanswered points past Les Garçons en Rose - though I decided in the circumstances it would not be prudent to tell her that) of screeching abuse… she called me **un rosbif imbecile -** whatever that is.

Not a compliment, peut-être? Unless she thinks I have the finely-honed physique of a Hereford Bull, par chance?? If so, this compliment was quixotic, albeit somewhat surreal. Perhaps inspired by Seurat, whom she referenced several times in her MA Thesis on 'The pivotal and noble role of the feminine feline (you can tell she wrote it…) in the development of 19th Century French Art.'

In a vain attempt to inject some much-needed humour into this rapidly deteriorating situation, I thanked her profusely for her Seurat-inspired compliment, but discreetly mentioned that I failed to see the point of it, when she was otherwise abusing me.

This attempt at la drôlerie du rosbif was met with possibly the greatest shower of venomous arrows since those faced by Achilles. Alas, I discovered *plus vite* that her own Achilles' heel was that she possessed no sense of irony whatsoever.

Her parthian shot was this (why couldn't Cupid shoot an arrow into *her* vituperative heart?): she told me in her most haughty Parisienne accent that I was no better than any of the other in-bred, lowlife moggies from Angleterre and that I did not appreciate the enormous effort required each night to look stunningly elegant and beautiful. I did wonder at this stage if she was a reincarnation of Marie Antoinette, but discretion got the better of valour and I declined to suggest this.

Alas, Fanny is now besotted with a Thai Boxing Bengal Cat from Marseille adorned, no doubt, with a bling bling 24-carat gold flea collar. He is probably a low life moggy whose FCH is a French-Algerian drug dealer with halitosis - *due to the excessive use of harissa* - and they say money can't buy class…

26th: *Papillon* is released early from jail for good behaviour, plus the Judge had decided that, with hindsight, he had been slightly hard on le rosbif.

## Captain Bligh and Fletcher Christian Volunteer for the RNLI

Having somehow survived the latest trip to France, Papillon had a brainwave and decided to volunteer for the RNLI - even though the Yorkshire Coast is about 70 miles away. It did seem a very noble thing to do, though I wouldn't fancy anyone's chances of survival if they were relying on him driving all the way to Scarborough, bearing in mind he would want to anchor at York to sail around the *MacArthur Glen Designer Outlet* for at least 3 hours.

We were both sitting in what he calls his study (FHM, GQ?) looking at the RNLI website in awe.

He told me that every member of the RNLI is an unpaid volunteer.

*'Seems fair enough to me…'* I thought. *'Our greatest ever naval hero, Lord Nelson, had a similar approach to ratings in the Royal Navy, until the mutiny of 1798.'*

'So are most of them press-ganged into service?' I asked. 'And what happens if they are late for training? Are they flogged with a cat o' nine tails?' which received the curt response of:

'Don't be so bloody stupid,' – a reply that didn't actually answer either of my questions.

I looked carefully at the RNLI website but there was no mention of flogging or getting a daily ration of rum - but I put that down to yet more budget cutting by the miserly Coalition Government.

I was then told by Captain Bligh that these supremely altruistic, brave men and women get no funding whatsoever from the Government - which seems as parsimonious an attitude as his own regarding my cat food.

'Can't they get an EU Grant…?' I asked, apparently naively. Ditto his uncouth retort, which again failed to answer my question.

*I hope they don't have to sit IQ Tests, otherwise he's got no chance*, I thought, disdainfully.

'Or why not let the Germans run it? They would then get millions of Euros each year in subsidies, although a wolf pack of RNLI U-Boats may not be the best way to spend the budget.'

For some reason, he just snorted, rolled his eyes and shook his head which led me to think...

*'Perhaps the East Yorkshire Seafaring Maisonettes have their own fleet of lifeboats?'*

After another 5 minutes, I said that if he volunteers - then so shall I.

'Oh yeah, what as?' hardly the response of the leader of a press gang.

**'The Mouser!'** I said with my chest puffed out with pride.

However, by this time, the atmosphere had become rather tense.
Then he told me that he intends to apply, but only as an Officer...

'I am sure that I would make an excellent RNLI Officer.'

And he thinks I'm stupid...

'I do not wish to take the wind out of your billowing sails but, to be frank, I think that if the RNLI were so desperate as to make you a Lieutenant, then that would lead to the first mutiny on an RNLI Lifeboat since its inception in 1824.'

Brutal, but honest, and at least I answered *his* question.

By now, the tension was simmering and I awaited his next, predictable shot across my bows.

We then looked at the RNLI 'How To Join' web page and my enthusiasm, I am ashamed to admit, started to sink quicker than the Titanic after it had hit the iceberg.

Imagine, for a moment, that you're part of the crew on a lifeboat.

Great! So far so good. Mouser Nelson is ready for action.

It's 2.30 a.m. (in the morning???) in freezing January (would it be possible to just enlist for the summer months on a nice sunny day?) and the pager's just woken you from a deep sleep in a snug, warm bed / bean bag.

You then head out to sea in complete darkness (no lights? Must be due to budget cuts) and 10m (not 10 millimeters by any chance???) waves rise and fall around you, ready to swamp you at any moment. (Maybe U-boats aren't such a bad idea after all.) Strong gale force winds throw the lifeboat around like a toy. (This doesn't sound like fun to me.) A fishing trawler is in difficulty 23 miles out to sea. (Can't they just hang on till it's light and the weather picks up?)…

Still want to volunteer? Possibly not.
Read on… Does the weather improve?

The crew members need to:

be over 17 (with the permission of parents) or over 18 years old.

'That knocks you out straightaway', hissed Bligh.

be under 45 years old (inshore lifeboat) or 55 (all-weather lifeboat).

pass a medical and eyesight test.

be physically fit.
'Well that knocks you out…' replied Christian.

live and/or work close to a lifeboat station.

'That knocks us both out…'

pass a probationary period that usually lasts for one year.

be a team player and be accepted by the rest of the crew. 'That also knocks you out…'

enjoy hard physical work.
'As does that…'

get on well with other people.
'And that..'

communicate easily.
'Not communicating at all would be far better in your case…'

obey orders when required.

'Obey orders? **Obey orders...?** That, above all else, makes you totally unsuited to life in the RNLI.'.

With the smug grin becoming of a tyrant of the seven seas, he then proceeded to complete his online application. Having assassinated my character, which I thought was grossly unfair and partially unfounded; he kicked me out of his *cabin*.

I had nothing else to do, so I decided to practice my rigging / climbing skills using the velvet curtains in the salon.

For this supposedly mutinous act, I was banished from the house for 10 days, which meant that I missed the opportunity to accompany him on his RNLI Training Course in Poole.

The RNLI's newest volunteer returned earlier than expected.

It was decided by mutual consent that perhaps he was not cut out to be a Guardian Angel of the Seas on account of:

1. His latent fear of heights... which became apparent when he had to jump into the pool.
2. His swimming skills being restricted to the 'doggy paddle' - which caused him to go round and round in ever-decreasing circles.
3. His allergic reaction to the rubber suits.
4. His inability to see in the dark and...
5. The wave generator caused him to be seasick, just after he had clambered inside a life raft with four other trainees - one of whom wanted to throw him back out. The Training Team did, however, thank him for trying and appreciated his

efforts and it was agreed the best way he could help their noble cause would be to continue donating and buying various items from the RNLI Shop. So, hopefully, I might get an RNLI Calendar and milk bowl for Christmas.

## Abandon Hope All Ye Who Enter A Dalliance With Good Looooordy Hair Removal Gel

This may be of particular interest to South American Death Squads, the International Triathlon Federation, Saddo-Masochists, the Egyptian Secret Police and the Yorkshire Space Exploration Programme:

Inspired by the smooth-limbed participants of the Tour de France, Rick Hinault purchased a 750 ml tube of *Good Looooordy Hair Removal Gel* from *Amazon*, immediately awarding it five stars. Like a doping-exempt masseur from the Highasakita Cycling Team, and with his arms going faster than the wings of a bumblebee on amphetamines, he enthusiastically smeared the honey-like gel all over his legs without first reading the warning that it should be rinsed off within six minutes and, ***under no circumstances whatsoever***, be left on for more than ten minutes after application.

Precisely eighteen minutes after application of the afore-mentioned gel he shot through the roof, beseeching me to not forget to water the plants and to immediately call the Police, the St John's Ambulance, his solicitor, the local Priest and the entire West Yorkshire Fire Brigade, as he hurtled towards the Moon by what remained of the shredded seat of his pants.

I don't think he could have flown any higher had *NASA* fired a rocket up his a\*\*\* (his words not mine: he clearly failed to wax lyrical…). Since returning to earth he has walked with a rather quaint and fetching gait that could be best described as a cross between John Wayne after 10 weeks in the saddle and a goose-stepping Adolf Hitler on anabolic steroids.

For five days after the Epilatoralypse he did nothing but rant and rave incoherently about a recurring nightmare re being attacked by Yul Brynner, Nosferatu, all the mutants from 'I am Legend' and 6,000 Mongolian Brick Headbutting Grasshopper Warrior Monks.

A week later he had finally recovered sufficiently to take me for my annual check-up at my local Veterinary Hospital, Drs. Snippet & See, where I met a flirtatious Sphinx from Dublin called Sinead and we agreed to meet up. I was still pining for Fanny so I thought an evening with a minx Sphinx would be a most agreeable way to help me overcome my recent loss. This was the first time I had met a Sphinx and did not realise they had no fur.

We got on like my human's kneecaps on fire eleven minutes after his initial, exploratory dabs of *Good Loooordy* but at the end of the evening she told me I was a little too furry for her, which I thought was going a bit beyond the pale. I was a sea of desolation until I remembered his tube of *Good Loooordy Hair Removal Gel* which he kept in his bathroom cabinet and was now using to burn alive the rats in our cellar.

She agreed to meet again around midnight that Friday for a valedictory saucer. So two hours before our midnight rendezvous, as I was ***absolutely determined*** to make a lasting impression, I sat on the sink in the bathroom, opened up the tube and spread some of the rodent-incinerating gel on the bottom of my paws, in my ears and on the end of my walrus-like whiskers (as she uncharitably described them). I diligently rinsed off the gel after five minutes then sat back to admire my semi-Sphinx appearance in the mirror for what I estimated to be no more than ten minutes.

Unfortunately, I had forgotten to replace the cap and, as I down sat on the tube, the remainder of the contents had spread all over my hindquarters. I only had myself to blame as I was too busy narcissistically admiring my new look to notice the gentle waft of smouldering fur. I was now about to experience first-hand the ineluctable and unforgettable 'perils of vanity'. All I could gasp before take-off was *'Hell hath no fury as a tube of Good Looooordy Hair Removal Gel scorned'*.

As my eyes widened to the size of two Wedgwood dinner plates and tears streamed down my crimson-coloured cheeks so much that my face resembled twin Niagara Falls, I soared upwards through the recently repaired hole in the roof ruminating that being attacked by six squadrons of kamikaze frelons would have been unbridled ecstasy compared to the fire & brimstone impact of this napalmesque gel.

I shot through the sky amid numerous reports of a yodelling, cat-like shooting star and others of a pre-emptive missile attack launched by Scottish Nationalists (by the more paranoid residents of Leeds), petrified that this could be a new form of neutering.

As I flew over the North Sea at the speed of Mach 1.8 towards Scandinavia, I screamed past a Sukhoi Su-24 of the Russian Federation Air Force heading in the general direction of the Arctic Circle. Its startled crew, which comprised of a somewhat hungover Pilot, Major Nikolai Buzzov, and his slightly incompetent Navigator, Senior Lieutenant Alexander Garminski, stared at me with wide-eyed, jaw-dropping incredulity as I shot past in two shakes of what was left of my afterburning tail.

The disorientated Navigator Garminski decided that what zoomed past at Mach 1.8 must have been an F-14 VL (Variant Literal) Tomcat brought back into service by the US Navy. This did at least take his mind off the fact that he was supposed to be directing his senior, and highly unimpressed, comrade towards the Latvian coastline en route to the Levashevo Air Base at St. Petersburg.

Major Buzzov and Senior Lieutenant Garminksi shook hands, as neither felt inclined to raise a toast, and made a joint oath to never again drink a bottle of vodka prior to embarking on a reconnaissance mission over the Baltic Sea, moments before ejecting.

As I entered Norwegian Airspace I passed four Valkyries riding the other way, no doubt searching for anyone who dared to use *Good Loooordy Hair Removal Gel* on more than two parts of their anatomy at once. I eventually crash-landed in a fjord 80 kilometres beyond the coast of Norway and the 8 degree Celsius water finally gave much-needed succour to my frazzled hindquarters.

Luckily a small colony of friendly Japanese Macaques (whose crimson faces matched my own), which had escaped from Trondheim Zoo in 2007 and were now permanent residents of the fjord, kindly dragged me out of the water when they realised I was neither a flying Eurasian Lynx nor a double-headed dragon: they had enough problems as it was with the local wolves, Chinese Tourists and Danish Triathletes.

The next day I managed to crawl to the safety and relative comfort of a remote outpost of the Royal Norwegian Marines. As soon as its commander Fenrik Magnus Trollengaard finally accepted that I was not a Russian Blue Spy, I was adopted as the platoon mascot-cum-living example of the effects of phosphorous grenades. I was also employed by the Veterinary School of the University of Oslo as an example of the perils of botched neutering by incompetent vets.

So every tube of *Good Looooordy Hair Removal Gel* has a silver lining as I was given a heated bean bag, fresh goat's milk and smoked Norwegian salmon every day, and was asked to write about my self-propelled flight through space by an avuncular Professor of Astrophysics, Dr. Benny Olaf Bunsenbernassen.

Sadly, after almost three weeks of this agreeable sojourn his eagle-eyed assistant, Mollie Kuulsen MSc, spotted my ear tag. After confirming my UK residence, they disconsolately arranged to fly me back to England despite the desperate and undignified exhortations of the catphobic Rick Hinault that they keep me permanently in Scandinavia. He even promised to cover the cost of granting me Norwegian Citizenship and a lifetime's supply of reindeer meat for myself, Dr. Bunsenbernassen's pet husky and Ms. Kuulsen's pet Norwegian Forest Cat if they acquiesced. With heavy hearts, they told me they felt compelled to send me back out of Nordic honour. I replied that, as far as I was concerned, they could be as dishonourable as they wished but as I may as well have been pleading with two Valkyries: I was destined for the Yorkshire Valhalla.

Upon my return to the UK, I went onto the Amazon website in order to award *Good Looooordy Hair Removal Gel* 125 stars. I hope to never meet a Sphinx again.

# October

**Artistic Licence**

The 2012 Tour Winner and Olympic Gold Medallist - the über-cool cycling cat Wiggo - having bravely come back from a broken collarbone the previous year, is knocked off his bike by some careless woman who later said that she simply did not see our modish, national hero. So should our mod-hero have done more to make his presence even more obvious?

Still, it could have been worse… it could have been a politician that mowed him down. More precisely, the type that claims £325,017.45 per annum in garden maintenance expenses for a 46th floor apartment in Islington. And when quizzed, with steely, resolve, insists all of their expense claims are perfectly legitimate and justified. *So how dare anyone question their moral fibre?* Maybe Robespierre wasn't so bad…even though he was a lawyer.

Why can't drivers of 4-wheeled vehicles just be more aware of cyclists?

So, I conducted some pondering 'outside the tray' and have come up with some ideas which could have made him more obvious:

Continuously ring a giant-size, 75cm bicycle bell.

Install a pedal-powered music system with two huge speakers on the handle bars and a sub-woofer on the rear mudguard playing The Jam and The Who at maximum volume.

Persuade the peloton to ride behind him all the time, even if just going out to buy some bread and milk. The Chorley branch of Maurice and Sons may, however, need to expand the number of bicycle parking bays in its car park and stock up on anti-chafing gel & isotonic sports drinks.

Only ever go out on his bike in his maillot jaune.

Or he could go one cadence further and grow his sideburns until they reach the tarmac… dye them bright yellow then wax them with such intensity that they develop a rigor mortis-like ability to stand parallel to the ground – and then place flashing beacons at each end…

Or, better still, he could ride a custom-built tandem bike so a mezzo-soprano could sit at the front singing various opera arias whilst he could be pedalling melodiously at the rear. This would have the additional benefit of making it easier to persuade the promising young riders in Team Gazolio-La Scala (Rossini, Donizetti, Girozzola and Pelotonetti) to cycle in the Lancashire Dolimites.

Two days later, Shane Sutton (if Wiggo is the Black Prince of British Cycling then he is undoubtedly its Edward III) is run over whilst out on his bike - then Cav has an accident on his bike in Italy when a car in front of him suddenly slams on its brakes (and I cynically thought that Italian drivers never bothered using their brakes…).

Side note: Richard II, who was the grandson of Edward III, introduced cutlery to the royal court. Admittedly not as spectacular as winning the battles of Crècy and Poitiers, but he would be mortified at the lack of progress over 700 years if he were to venture into any 21$^{st}$ century fast-food outlet.

But what is going on? By now, Froomie and El Cyclo Supremo must be wondering if they are next. If I were them, I would stay at home and train on a Watt Bike. Much safer.

Bit strange this, they're all members of *Team Sky*: the winners of the 2012 Tour.

Personally, I can sniff some possible, substance-enhanced, (and I don't mean flea drops mixed with absinthe) skulduggery here…

El Cyclo Supremo, not surprisingly, calls for car and lorry drivers to be more aware of, and considerate towards cyclists.

Why can't we learn from the Dutch and have dedicated lanes and traffic lights for cyclists? How much more popular would cycling be if people knew it was safe for them or their children to go out on the road? How healthier and fitter would *les rosbifs* be if they exercised more, whilst enjoying the great outdoors on a Bianchi?

Alas, when I heard the 2014 TDF was going to start in Leeds, all I could think of was *mass peloton armageddon* before they even reach Otley, in which case the Government should be building new hospitals and employing more nurses. I think the winner of the 2014 TDF will truly be the 'last man standing' and any national anthems will have to be replaced by the funeral march.

**Embellishing Romeo's Profile**

The Lonesome Cowboy was becoming disillusioned with the few women he had met via the Internet cattle market and their 'creative descriptions' of themselves.

Here are some examples of embellishments which would have impressed Miss Havisham:

Moderate build = obese.
Curvaceous = clinically obese.
Weight '…would rather not say' = even fatter than curvaceous.
Looks are important = not if you earn over £100,000 p.a.
Looks 'very attractive' = had plastic surgery and botox.
Looks 'I'm hot' = had plastic surgery, botox and breast implants.
Don't mind if you smoke = she smokes likes a chimney.
Occasional drinker = borderline alcoholic.
Light drinker = alcoholic.
Moderate drinker = raving alcoholic.
Non-drinker = in rehab.
Tattoos = N/A (a walking canvas).
Job = Doctor/Medical (receptionist in a clinic).
Education = University of Life (Divorced at least 3 times, hence expert in Family Law)
Likes going to the gym = went once 5 years ago and sat in the sauna for 3 hours.

So, I decided to help and accessed his emails when he went out on his latest date.

'She claims in her profile to be Japanese and an expert in jiu-jitsu and Kendo. Call the Police if I'm not back by midnight…'

This wasn't very reassuring – I thought that I would be better off calling the Police if he brings her back.

'…I hope she's not a bunny boiler.'

I wasn't quite sure what he meant by that phrase, but I thought I wouldn't mind that at all, as I loved the 'Lapin sauté aux herbes en Provence' that his neighbours cooked as a welcome home party after his release from prison.

Whilst he was out, I thought I would embellish Romeo's profile slightly, as follows:

Height = 5' 1" (same height as a Sumatran Tiger: that will impress the ladies).

Weight = 18 st 12 lbs (sign of a successful hunter, very impressive too).

Tattoos = inked all over (orange and black stripes).

Looks = 'I don't look great' (I'm afraid I've got to be brutally honest).

Exercise = jogging… my memory (if that…).

Heavy smoker (he does look debonair with a Cuban cigarillo).

Heavy drinker (that will appeal to everyone in Britain).

Favourite hobbies = Karaoke - especially Mozart. Watching paint dry. Train spotting.

Occupation = Tortured Genius (as he does look mentally retarded on his passport photo) and Management Guru in Positive *'Incompetence is merely a state of mind imposed by emotionally stunted martinets'* Thinking.

Income = Still looking for someone to give me a penny for my thoughts. (this will explain my diet of dry cat food). So destitute I can barely pay attention.

Favourite Reading = (Book) 'How To Live In Harmony With Your Pet Komodo Dragon'.

Page 3 of the Sun.

Favourite pets = Komodo Dragons and Anacondas (make him seem less dull and boring).

SUMMARY - An existentialist couch potato who loves to live life in the bohemian fast lane (inspired by Paris). Looking for a refined & sophisticated lady who knows that *Perrier* is not French for 'Tap' who likes to keep fit, so an ex-member of the Russian Olympic Pole Vaulting Team would be most welcome and who, above all, loves cats and is vehemently opposed to the heinous practise of neutering. Dog owners and skimmed milk drinkers need not reply.

I then enjoyed the remainder of the evening lying back on my beanbag listening to some cool Miles Davis whilst reading about the history of Le Tour de France.

I had just finished climbing to the top of Mont Ventoux, picturing myself leading the peloton in a red and white polka dot jersey (or at least a polka dot flea collar) when in burst Romeo.

'I wonder who he has brought back this time?' I pondered gloomily '...she can only be an improvement on the previous ones.'

He sauntered into my kitchen grinning like a Cheshire Cat:
'Finally, Nelson, I think I may have met someone really nice. She is polite, pleasant and not obsessed with how much money I earn, my socio-economic status, my postcode or whether I own my own house. And she **really is** Japanese. Doesn't drink much and doesn't smoke. She is a classically trained pianist and has three Degrees…'

'She sounds far too sophisticated, elegant and intelligent for you. I think you should stick to Morehopethanjoys.'

'She has her own business called… 'Yakuza Music' – at least that is what I think it is called.'

'Really? Are you sure you want to get involved with her?'

'She is trained in several types of Japanese Martial Arts, so you'd better be careful when you talk to her – don't be offensive. The only downside to her is that she has 3 cats. A 15 year old Siamese-Burmese cross, a 9 year old Turkish Van and a 3 year old Japanese Bobtail called Kiku which she told me is a girl's name.'

'*A 3 year old, **female** Japanese Bobtail?*' at this point, I stopped admiring the misty view from Le Col de Ventoux and started to pay attention.

'I'm delighted to say she has invited me to her house next Saturday for a Bonfire Night, Thai Beef Curry. **Unfortunately,** she asked if you would like to come too, as she has never met a British Shorthair before and she had heard they are - and I quote: '…a wonderful, loyal, loving, sweet-natured breed', but I told her Cromwell would not want to come…'

**'Cromwell???'**
'…as he only eats dry cat food so would not like Thai Beef Curry and he does not like Asian Cats invading his territory.'

'Perhaps you would like to inform your new Geisha Girlfriend that Prince Rupert would be absolutely delighted to accept her kind invitation. Having never tried Thai Cuisine before, he is looking forward to expanding his culinary horizon and meeting Kicker too... and if you lie to her and tell her that I did not want to come, then I shall have no choice but to make this known… if she ever comes here.'

A rapier was thus plunged through his devious hopes of excluding me from what could be a very nice soirée.

# November

**Bonfire Night**

The highlight of the month promises to be a Bonfire Night Thai Curry.

Being Catholics, we don't celebrate Bonfire Night and are of the opinion that if Guy Fawkes was to come back to life and blow up the Houses of Parliament today, he may be feted as a hero.

But this was a special evening, so I was combed, wormed and given a double dose of *Pink Sun 'Neem'* organic flea drops - then he sprayed something by *Jean-Paul Gaultier* all over me, which I must admit smelt much nicer than my 3-day old litter tray.

With me suitably coiffeured - like a Cavalier's Cat - we then set off. Thomas Blake Glover gave me multiple warnings:

'Behave impeccably as the Japanese are the politest people on earth. Resist the temptation to climb up any curtains, if bored. Plus, try not to upset anyone or anything.'

I was also told that the loyal human companion's name was Nene and the Bobtail was Kiku, rather than Kicker. Apparently, Nene comes from an old Samurai Clan, which I thought must explain her interest in Kendo. 'I bet she doesn't get many burglars...' thinking already that she was more useful than the useless, Swiss Army knife-wielding fool that I was lumped with.

The Siamese-Burmese was asleep and the Turkish Van had gone out, so it was just the four of us.

It was a very pleasant evening, although I could sense he was on tenterhooks, having never eaten with chopsticks before. Luckily, these were only required for the first course, as it was embarrassing watching him struggle to use them. I did try whispering to him: '…keep the bottom one still and just move the top one.' Unfortunately, he didn't hear me mention that I meant up & down and not side to side.

*Socially inept as ever, but can you really expect any better from an ex-jailbird…* I asked myself rhetorically. *I know that he knows that I know, he is dreading me mentioning anything about his incarceration in France - which will not go down terribly well with someone from such a high class background.*

It was a very nice evening, spent listening to classical music; her favourite composer being Mozart.

Despite embellishing his profile with hobbies, including classical music (I did tell him not to do it), this extended to *Nirvana* (being accompanied by a cellist) and *Roll Over Beethoven*. I could tell that he was dreading her asking him the obvious question, which occurred over dessert…

'I am very impressed that you are a member of MENSA. I find most people around here to be quite charming - but mentally defective. I have never come across so many village idiots in one place before.'

'I know, I don't like to boast about it, in case it intimidates people.'

*'Or… maybe because I told him what the answers were in each of the tests - as Pinocchio had no idea…'*

'I love Mozart's operas especially Cosi Fan Tutte. I think it is so lovely. What do you think?'

'Err… Cromwell likes Mozart much more than me. Don't you Oli?'

Oliver Cromwell hadn't been paying attention, on account of being held in a jiu-jitsu stranglehold by the tiny, trained assassin of a Bobtail, who was displaying her Martial Arts skills. When she asked me to stick out my right front paw, I did so, not expecting her to grab it, then twist her body round and throw me over her shoulder a dozen times, like a rag doll.
Luckily, I fell onto her bean bag, which cushioned my falls. This was not what I had anticipated as post-dinner entertainment.

'**Kiku**, let go of our esteemed guest. Can't you see that he can't breathe?'

She bowed apologetically (to her, not me, which I thought was a bit impolite, but I wasn't going to argue with her). This was tempered by being referred to as an esteemed guest. I've never been called that before.

Nene picked me up with the gentle hands of a Ninja Assassin and sat me on her lap, whilst Kiku launched herself at the unsuspecting and hitherto fast asleep Siamese-Burmese - practising her low and high roundhouse kicks on him - whilst he tried his best to defend himself with a cushion. Then her training came to an abrupt end when she was thrown outside.

'So Cromwell-san, your master (master?) tells me you love Mozart.'

Looking at the panic-stricken face of 'my master' who was clearly relying on me to get him out of this awkward situation, the Lord Protector calmly replied:

'Yes, I do indeed, especially the Impressionists and Dutch Masters. But I am not overly-fond of modern day stuff. I think it is talentless rubbish.'

She smiled serenely and said:
'It is true what they say about British Shorthairs. Intelligent and sophisticated. Humble and amusing too.'

I had no idea what she was going on about and Parliament just sat there shrugging his shoulders.

'Cromwell-san, I so love Cosi Fan Tutte. What about you?'

'I agree, it is lovely but, personally, I prefer rum 'n' raisin.'

Parliament collapsed with a groan of dismay, whilst she gave me a quizzical look, then started giggling.

The rest of the evening went without incident – we all listened to The Magic Flute - and it seemed, according to Nene, that I had played a major role in cementing their blossoming relationship.

He eventually told her that my real name was Nelson: he thought that if he referred to me as Cromwell it would be a nice surprise for her to learn how charming I was (which he said through gritted teeth). Amazingly, she believed him - unless she was just being polite.

Kiku had apparently taken a shine to me and was very keen to continue seeing me, which I agreed to, on condition that she did not beat me up again. Being a victim of domestic violence just the once was enough for me.

As the month progressed, he seemed to see more of her and, on one occasion, even I was invited where, to my immense relief, Kiku offered to teach me Haiku - which I promised to have a go at - if she promised not to strangle me, break my paws or subject me to any roundhouse kicks.

The only downside to the month was learning that many people were predicting the end of the world on December 21st. '*Typical, just as I finally meet a nice girl,*' we lamented in unison.

To understand better what will become of the world after the 21st we watched *'I Am Legend'*. We had to wait 5 years to watch this film, as my miserly LHC would only buy the DVD when it was on offer at £3. I was scared witless and tried vainly to cover my eyes with my paws - whilst hiding under my bean bag. So… these cannibalistic mutants will be all that is left of mankind?

He told me that they reminded him of his neighbours when he lived near Redfern Station in Sydney. No wonder he came back to England! Though he did say that The Rose Hotel in Chippendale was the best pub in the world, despite its lack of Trappist Beers. Maybe we could fly out on the 20th and seek sanctuary there?

I wish I was a leopard.
Decided to take up Krav Maga.

# December

**Last boat to Bugarach**

My LHC gave me a special treat - possibly a valedictory one with the 21st looming - a trip to see *Skyfall*.

Thoroughly enjoyed the film and my LHC and I both agree that Daniel Craig is the best James Bond since Sean Connery.

But... why is it that Bond's villains always have pet cats?

Matthew Flinders and Trim weren't villains, surely?

Why not a ferret, a guinea pig or a Vietnamese Pot-Bellied Pig?

I shall feel compelled to turn Sam Mendes down if he offers me a demeaning role as a villain's pet cat in the next 007 production.

It may have been subconsciously due to the fear of my impending demise, but I got very emotional watching the end of the film, which involves a sad scene with M, James Bond's mentor and boss. She brought him back from the abyss (and if it had been this Coalition Government, they would have made him redundant, reclaimed all his overseas expenses, taken away his pension, exchanged his Aston Martin for a Morris Minor and replaced him with a one-legged, transgender, Romanian Jobseeker - paying the minimum wage).

I couldn't stop howling, despite my LHC threatening to lock me out of the house for 3 days and bolting my cat flap. The rest of the audience were staring angrily at me and I overheard at least one less than sympathetic cinema goer impudently shout: 'Who let that bloody cat in?'.

I couldn't help myself, it was such a sad ending... when the closest you have been to raw feline emotion is watching repeat episodes of *Top Cat*... and it was such a waste of a classic car. Wanton destruction. Couldn't they just blow up a *2CV*? I reckon if Dr. Robert Neville had bombed around New York in an *Aston Martin DB5* in '*I Am Legend*' he would have survived and met someone like

Monica Bellucci. Then his only worry would have been if the leader of the hive of mutants had been someone like Vincent Cassel (who would make a Bond villain, par excellence).

I asked for an *Aston Martin DB5* for Xmas, instead of the usual multi-coloured ping-pong balls. A snip at just £84,995 (for a 2008 model).

5th-10th: Been writing what seems like 3,000 Xmas Cards to all my chums and family. I could have been out hunting rabbits. At times like this, I wish I was Jewish. Been tempted to bid a fond farewell to everyone and wondered whether they will get their cards before the 21st - otherwise this will have been a total waste of my *possibly limited time* on Earth.

Even sent a card to Fanny, though she will probably use it as bait for an unsuspecting rat.

11th-20th: Been checking out catteries in Bugarach. They are all full up with Russian Blues. First Chelsea - next Olympique Bugarach.

Really annoyed that the world is destined to end 4 days before I am due to get a new flea collar for Christmas. My LHC is even more annoyed, having booked a trip to Amsterdam in early January. He reckons Holland is really ****** (his words, not mine) as most of it is below sea level. Apparently, lots of Romanian immigrants have been busy dismantling the dykes and selling inflatable dinghies in the Rembrandtplein. As a result, all of Amsterdam's hotels have stopped, due to labour shortages in the kitchen and cleaning departments. But… pickpocketing has fallen to record lows outside Centraal Station.

21st (9.27 a.m.): Got a postcard from Fanny in Bugarach. She writes that it has an overwhelming sense of ennui, compared with the Latin Quarter and is full of very rich but anxious businessmen from Moscow with their pampered Russian Blue Cats.

I read that, despite averaging crowds of 120 people, the newly rouble-endowed Olympique Bugarach will be bidding for Messi and Neymar in the January transfer window and hoping to appoint José Movintoswsixinho as the new Manager.

Four Real Madrid players jump on the rouble-encrusted bandwagon, saying that it had always been their life-long ambitions to play for Berwick Rangers but, since BRFC cannot afford their wages, Olympique Bugarach run a close second.

Bugarach becomes the first hamlet in the world, which is nowhere near the sea, to have jetties built for a fleet of Russian yachts... just in case.

So... Fanny has now decided that British Shorthairs are not so bad after all - I just caught her on a bad day and she would like to invite me over for Boxing Day to make up - if the world survives Armageddon.

10 minutes later: I text her, saying how sorry I am to hear that her pugilistic Bengal has been neutered, but I have now met a sweet little Bobtail, who, despite being capable of killing me 9 times over, is very nice.

21st (8.24 p.m.): Try to relax with a John Coltrane CD and leap onto the kitchen worktop, only to find he has chucked out my CD Player and replaced it with an *iPod,* hence condemning my entire CD collection to the same scrapheap that I am due to be condemned to within 4 hours. To worsen my mental state, he is watching *'I Am Legend'* again.

21st (11:59 p.m.): Typical. The world is about to end, I am about to die and my miserable LHC has locked me in the kitchen - as punishment for being sick on his new Chinese Rug. Tried to explain that it was solely due to nerves, but to no avail. I hope he gets the norovirus.

My anxiety levels are now so high that I cease to be annoyed by the Xmas tinsel that my cretin of a LHC wrapped around my litter tray two days before, telling me that it would make a great Xmas photo for him to circulate via *Facebook* to *tout le monde* - with me sat in it; humiliated by a half-wit.

I am lying in my beanbag, or more precisely, under my beanbag, next to my tinsel-covered litter tray that has not been emptied for three days, awaiting the end.

I can honestly say that I am petrified and cannot help staring at the kitchen door, with eyes resembling giant milk saucers, as I await a hive of mutants from '*I Am Legend'* that will surely come bursting through my cat flap.

I have five ping pong balls lined up to fire at them, but that is my only line of defence as the fool upstairs - now drunkenly snoring in bed so loudly that any mutant north of Bordeaux will hear him - decided it would be a good idea to clip my claws for Christmas.

I do at least find a used 25cl. *Kronenbourg* beer bottle - which he had earlier drunkenly lobbed at the *Brabantia* bin and missed (useless to the end...) which I can wield in my defence. However, I doubt whether my last stand will be as glorious as that of the 300 at Thermopylae.

22$^{nd}$ (2:31 a.m.): My cat flap is still intact and my litter tray is now overflowing. Curiosity is killing me, so I gingerly poke my head out into the dark abyss outside. I look right, then left, then right again and see no sign of any mutants or Mayan Shamen.

Suddenly... I freeze with abject fear as I spot the Grim Reaper staring at me – he is standing just six feet away...

**This is it.... the end...**

But I calm down when I realise that it is just a garden gnome holding a pickaxe.

I do some yoga exercises for 15 minutes to get my heart rate back to normal - then collapse onto my bed, mentally exhausted.

22$^{nd}$: Day One - post-apocalypse.

It is still raining.

The closest the UK has had to the apocalypse is 140 flood warnings, so I have decided that global warming is a myth. I am expecting an influx of Turkish Vans.

Wiggo has recovered from his broken rib and is justly voted the *BBC Sports Personality of the Year*. I was half-expecting him not to be given his award with the Duchess of Cambridge explaining retrospectively that: *'I'm really sorry, I simply did not see him…'* having instead given the award to one of the ceremony's presenters for winning the 2012 BBC Subbuteo Tournament against the pundits of Match of the Day (MOTD 1 and 2).

The 2014 Tour de France will start in that famous French Département just north of Normandy called… Yorkshire.

We are still alive, no one from Team Sky has been run over recently, and all is well. Superstitious idiots around the world will now be eating nothing but baked beans for the next 13 years.

Property prices have plummeted in the Pyrenees and the festive season is upon us.

To my dismay, I read that one of my Antipodean pen pals had questioned my nationality. I would have thought that being named Nelson might have provided a clue *par excellence* to my heritage.

If I was a Russian Blue, my name would more likely be Kutuzov, Kuznetsov, Kerensky or Raskolnikov, *perchance*. Similarly, if I was a Chartreux, I would be named after a French hero such as Montcalm, Lafayette, Ney or Jean-Paul Belmondo. Or if I was a Spotted Mist I would be named after an Australian hero such as Cook, Flinders, Macquarie or Tatiana Grigorieva.

The world did not end and so I can look forward to an apocalyptic-free 2013.

**31st December:**

Absolutely delighted to hear that Wiggo has just been Knighted. Even more delighted that the Queen did not behead him with her sword; apologising after the ceremony: *'I am terribly sorry, I simply did not see him…'*

Not sure whether that was for winning Le Tour de France, winning Gold at the London Olympics, or resisting the temptation - hence dashing the hopes of 62 million Frenchmen - to sing the Belgian National Anthem in Paris.

## January

### The Night Watch and The Potato Eaters

As a special treat, my LHC takes me on a weekend trip to Amsterdam and we fly with *KLM;* much more of a pleasant experience than flying *Harp Air*. Even though the plane seemed to go up then go down again, we still got a snack and coffee (for FREE).

Amsterdam is a very pleasant city, though full of those annoyingly stupid German toy dogs called Snorterz (they may be an appropriate breed for this city with all of its hash cafes). Despite Amsterdam dripping in history, fine art and architectural wonders, my LHC just wanted to visit the Red Light District and try some skunk - which did make me wonder what he wanted to do with an odoriferous ferret.

One highlight of my trip was visiting the Hermitage Museum, which temporarily housed the Van Gogh Exhibition. I was amazed at how prolific Vincent was and admired his landscapes as much as his later work. Yet he never sold one painting during his short life. No wonder he was so angry all of the time. It also explained why his paintings - such as *The Potato Eaters* - consisted largely of different shades of brown: the impoverished wretch obviously could not afford to buy colours such as vermilion.

The museum made a huge fuss about Van Gogh deciding to crop one of his ears. I couldn't understand why they did this, as the Germans regularly crop the ears (both not just one) of Doberman Pinschers. He must have looked slightly ridiculous with just one cropped ear. Perhaps it was Gauguin's idea which, in hindsight, must have upset him.

We also went to the Rijksmuseum which housed the 17th Century Dutch Masters (artists, not footballers). Many of the paintings seemed to be of battle scenes between the Dutch and British Navies. The painting I was looking forward to seeing the most - but which I was rather disappointed with - was The Company of Captain Frans Banning Cocq and Lieutenant Willem van Ruytenburch preparing to march out… but this is more often referred to by philistines like my LHC, as The Night Watch.

Having spent almost an hour queuing to get to the front of the admiring crowd (I found the Italians to be the loudest and rudest visitors), I managed to look up at the canvas, which was so huge that I had to stand up on my rear legs (my front legs in front of me at 90 degrees to the floor for balance).

So… I was standing there, thinking how difficult it was to make out the faces of the arquebusiers in the painting (other than the two officers) and I would have been aggrieved at the time had I paid 100 Guilders to be portrayed with a grey face. No wonder his career went downhill after that.

Whilst I was ruminating van Rijn's decision to sacrifice commercial gain for artistic pedantry, a loud, fat, ill-mannered Italian walked into me, knocking me forward beyond the tripwire. Luckily, it wasn't mined and I had learned how to roll in my Aikido lesson. I managed to execute a roundhouse kick to his shin, causing him to fall over the tripwire, cursing in Italian - for which he was ejected.

I then sauntered off to enjoy the rest of the exhibition and received polite applause from a group of Japanese visitors who clearly also had enough of the rude Italians. To my surprise, the Philistine had been sitting outside for 2 hours, looking agitated, having sprinted through the whole museum in less than half an hour.

'I was bored stiff. All we've done today is look at art galleries. I've seen some nice bars round here, so let's go and get a beer then we can visit the Red Light District. Now that should be much more fun. That is what Amsterdam is all about…'

I sighed, resigning myself to what could have been - had Nene and Kiku been with us.

I thought the Red Light District was highly over-rated and he insisted that we pop into a hash café, where I instantly collapsed upon entering, due to the fumes. We also came across some bizarre shops with what looked like spiky cat collars, whips and leather masks - all for humans... Weirdest looking stuff I'd ever seen.

We did find a very nice, traditional bar, which seemed to have a 'stuffed cat' on a bookshelf...

'That's how you'll end up, if you're not careful', he said, which I thought was totally uncalled for.

Moreover, there was a live cat helping the barman, plus another bar that specialised in Belgian Beers - although he only stayed for one 'due to the exorbitant prices'.

Overall, a nice trip, even though the food was terrible and expensive - and everything came with frites and mayonnaise.

**Celtic Connections**

Our Amsterdam trip was quickly followed by a trip to Glasgow to see Celtic Connections.

The highlight was a concert celebrating the traditional music of Scotland.

My LHC was looking forward to listening to a divine Gaelic chanteuse, having recently bought her enchanting CD, which I am sure he said was entitled 'I Am Yum'. Must admit, I thought this an excellent idea - combining music with food.

It was when we were getting ready to go to the concert that he produced my Xmas Gift: a tartan flea collar, which I thought would be fine if I was a Scottish Rex or my name was Rob Roy. He also gave me a new dose of *Pink Sun 'Neem'* organic flea drops and a spray of *JPG*.

He put the flea collar on me, but seemed somewhat disappointed that I wasn't dancing a highland reel with excitement at being adorned with said ornament.

'Don't you like it?'

'Well, perhaps it would look better if you could spike up the fur on the top of my head - then I might resemble Rod Stewart.'

The fool looked at me for a moment, then decided this was an excellent idea, so he got some hair gel.

Five minutes later, I was walking along Sauchiehall Street looking like a Caledonian punk rocker.

To add to my embarrassment, he had bought himself a Tam O'Shanter and a pair of (predominantly yellow) Buchanan tartan trews, as he wanted to look the part and fit in with the locals.

'Like naming your house in France '*Agincourt*'?'

'That was your idea! I knew I shouldn't have listened to you. That porcelain house sign, which was hand painted in Limoges, cost me €250.'

We got to the concert hall and were eagerly awaiting the combined singing/cookery class.

They even announced it was going to be a great evening of 'garlic music' celebrating the garlic language and garlic culture. I never knew the Scots were so fond of garlic. I was surprised to see that we were the only two people in the entire audience wearing tartan: and we were Sassenachs.

The comperes of the show came on stage and started talking double-dutch. Someone later said they were talking in *Garlic* which at least was consistent with the culinary theme. Although we had front row seats, I couldn't understand a word of what they were saying.

Every now and then, they would make a witty garlic aside, and although they found it hysterically funny, no one else in the auditorium made a murmur. 'Dour Scots' I assumed.

After 20 minutes of their effective soliloquy, the first act came on. He was a chap from New York who played the bagpipes and wore *Levi Jeans*. I had to ask whether Scotland had recently declared war on the USA and launched a pre-emptive strike on its Eastern Seaboard; but I was told to be quiet. I also thought he could have made a bit more effort sartorially, unless denim was a cowboy tartan.

After a few minutes, he went off and we sat back, looking forward to non-stop Gaelic music.

On the train up to Glasgow I had asked whether Martyn Bennett would be playing, having enjoyed listening to his brilliant CD '*Grit*', but was told that sadly he had died of cancer a few years ago at the tender age of 33.

Unfortunately, the comperes came back on for another 15 minutes, again talking double-Dutch - then occasionally speaking in English. Each time they departed the stage, a new act would come on. This went on all evening and eventually the singing chef came on - but she was only allowed to perform an Entrée of one song, before being forced to make way for the Masters of Ceremony.

It was like the Highland Clearances had begun again.

I did mention to Bonnie Prince Charlie next to me that she was close enough for me to spring up on stage and ask her to sign my copy of '*I Am Yum*' or at least give me the traditional recipe for porridge, but I was told to shut up.

The concert eventually finished near to midnight, by which time all of the restaurants and pubs had shut - even though it was a Saturday evening.

'That's Lowlanders for you. They should have held the concert in Inverness. I bet they'll be celebrating into the wee hours of the morning there.'

We eventually found one pub where he had a pint of 80 Shilling. He must have been desperate for a beer, as that was even more outrageous than the prices in the Belgian Bar in Amsterdam.

Celtic were not playing in Glasgow that weekend, so we instead went to the Kelvingrove Gallery - which was much more to his liking, as it was full of weapons.

The highlight of the weekend, after the disappointment of the Celtic Connections concert, was finding a very snazzy bike shop in the West End called '*Siempre*' that was also a café-bar.

My only criticisms of this fine and friendly establishment were that they had no cat litter facilities and no Miles Davis playing in the background.

Otherwise it was the best coffee shop we had ever been in, even better than any in Sydney according to my LHC, and only the risk of missing our train back to England stopped *le blaireau rosbif* from buying yet more cycling jerseys.

We had been warned that Glasgow was the roughest place in the British Isles; plagued with poverty, criminal gangs and religious hatred - but we found it to be bohemian, with very nice architecture, made from red stone, and the people were charming... even though I couldn't understand much of what they were saying. Certainly much friendlier than Edinburgh, whose snooty residents couldn't be any colder if they were entombed in ice.

In fact, all of the Glasgow lassies kept commenting on how dapper I looked in my Rod Stewart flea collar and how irresistible my LHC looked in his Buchanan Tartan Trews. They said something along the lines of him looking like '*a wee Scotty Rupert the Bear*' before falling about laughing.

We both agreed that if our favourite French restaurant in Leeds (le magnifique *Kendell's Bistro* - which has to deserve at least one chef's hat, so the Head Chef can wear one), ever relocates to Glasgow, then we would emigrate to Scotland. I have already told my LHC that I would like a *Kendell's Bistro* Cookery Book for next Christmas - if they could please publish one.

**A Night At The Opera**

In an uncharacteristic moment of generosity, my LHC decided, inspired by his new found love of opera, or his new found desire to impress his new found Japanese girlfriend Nene… to treat us all to a night out at the very impressive, King Harold Opera House in Godwinson-upon-Ouse to watch a production of Puccini's '*Madama Butterfly*'. I think it was also a way to sweeten the pill, as he had failed to tell her that he organised for the British half of this opera-going foursome to go up to see his old drinking pal in Sunderland the following weekend and watch Berwick Rangers vs. Rangers.

He was clearly trying to impress Nene by insisting on '…having a pre-dinner apéro'.

'As opposed to a post-dinner apéro?'
I enquired, which resulted in being threatened with expulsion if I continued to make any more impudent comments.

My entire collection of Ryuichi Sakamoto CDs miraculously became **his** collection, and were laid out in order on the coffee table, for when Nene and Kiku turned up.

Perpetrating a brazen deception, he had cleaned out my litter tray *and* washed it, put out a saucer of my favourite Jersey Cream (covering it with cling film, so I couldn't spoil his deception by drinking it), plus a king-sized tin of *Cat Master Chef* Coq au Vin (similarly covered in cling film) and 4 brand new ping pong balls.

'Who are you expecting… Jane Fonda?'

As soon as the doorbell sounded, Sakamoto-san's mournful song about an appropriately throbbing heart started to play - on cue with the precision of an NVA Brass Band. And, as Jane and her Bobtail demurely strolled in, I was busy quartering limes for 'his & hers' apéritifs of caipirinhas.

I was summoned to the front door to re-introduce myself, which I did with alacrity, after raking over my litter tray one last time, knowing that my favourite Japanese Bobtail would be accompanying us to the opera.

'Nene, you may remember, Nelson… the cat that I inherited upon my divorce.'

Charming.

'Yes, I do indeed. He is such a handsome cat and what a splendid name for a noble British breed.'

Well, thank you.

'I think my Kiku has already taken quite a shine to him.'

Me too, as long as she doesn't practice her jiu-jitsu moves on me again.

'She's more than welcome to have him… just joking'.

Many a true sentiment said in jest.
'Is it really true that he can speak English?'

And French.

'I'm afraid so, as you'll no doubt learn to your cost.'

No, she's nice.

'Ah, I really like your sense of humour. Nelson looks like butter would not explode in his mouth. Can he speak Japanese too? I remember you telling me that you spent 5 years learning Japanese and all you can remember is 'biru san-bon douzo'. That was so funny that I emailed my parents in Osaka. My father thinks you are a half-wit. Your sense of humour is so charming!'

'Despite being able to speak English he is still just a **stupid cat** with a brain the size of a cherry blossom. Ha ha. Go on Nelson, why don't you say 'Hello' to our esteemed guests… in Japanese?'

Having maintained a samurai-like, dignified silence at this shower of barbed comments, I promptly did as I was told:

Good evening, Ladies.
Ojo-sama gata, konbannwa.
お嬢様方、こんばんわ

It is my ineluctable pleasure to make your enchanting acquaintances again.
Anatagatato miwakutekini saikaidekitakotoha
watakushinitotte shigokuno yorokobi to zonjimasu。

あなた方と魅惑的に再会できたことは、私にとって至極の喜びと存じます。

May I please re-introduce myself?
Saido jiko-syokai shite yoroshiidesyo ka。
再度自己紹介してよろしいでしょうか。


I am Nelson, top cat of this fine abode.
Nelson to moushimasu。　Kono ryouke ni kyojyu suru oyabunn　no　neko desu。
ネルソンと申します。この良家に居住する親分の猫です。


Would you care for some jersey cream par écheance?
Moshikashite jersey cream wo sukoshi gosyomi nasaimasu ka。
もしかしてジャージークリームを少しご賞味なさいますか。


You are a veritable pair of chrysanthemums as true as my loyal human companion is a venus fly trap.
Watashi no tyusei na ningen no kompanion ga haetori-gusa de　aruno ga shin no gotoku、anatagata ha shinn no kiku no tsugai de irassyaimasu。
私の忠誠な人間のコンパニオンがハエ取り草であるのが真のごとく、あなたがたは真の菊のつがいでいらっしゃいます。

**'All right. You can stop showing off now.'**

Despite being rudely interrupted by my fellow host, I completed my warm greetings thus:

Please forgive my loyal human companion.
Douka, watashi no tyusei na companion wo oyurushi kudasai。
どうか、私の忠誠な人間のコンパニオンをお許しください。

He is just a half-wit.
Tadano manuke desu。
ただの間抜けです。

Kiku then purred something to Nene who politely covered her mouth with her hand, as she giggled:

'I am sorry but Kiku is very cheeky. She was born in Pontefract. She says she agrees wholeheartedly with my father and she thinks that if your cat really has a brain the size of a cherry blossom, then yours can surely be no greater than that of a grain of rice… isn't it nice that we all share your sense of humour?'

Absolutely.

By this point, Kiku was lying on her back, shaking gently with her paw politely covering her mouth.
**'Right then, caipirinhas anyone?'**
I was on caipirinha-making Chief Assistant duty for my opera ticket Quid Pro Quo (which put me off going, to be honest, as I could not imagine the

cacophonous sound of electric guitars being suitable for a Puccini opera: Wagner's *'Die Walküre'* perhaps?). At least he didn't want to impress her - on account of being accused of cat cruelty - with his boring party trick of crushing ice by placing some cubes under my bean bag - then dropping me onto them.

'What if she doesn't like them?' I had cautiously asked Ricardinho dos Samba Bossa Nova…

'Don't be so negative. Why do you always have to rain on my parade? Everyone likes my expertly crafted caipirinhas (failing to acknowledge my Zen master lime chopping capabilities). These are bound to impress her, so **don't cock it up for me by ruining the evening.**'

*Douzo, I was only trying to help*, I thought to myself, thinking she was the nicest girl he had come across in 12 months of Psycho Dating. And, more importantly, I was hoping to create a good impression on Kiku the Japanese Bobtail (the Japanese Bobtail equivalent of Koyuki Kato - which I thought was a most apt name).

Being a well-bred Japanese, Nene felt duty bound not to offend her fawning host (him, not me) by refusing his kind offer of a caipirinha. I felt duty bound to tell the Divine Fawner that I would like to extend our hospitality to her Bobtail by removing the cling film covering the cream and Coq au Vin…

'Otherwise I'll tell them the truth that for 365 days a year I am force-fed a constipation-inducing diet of dry cat food.'

So, he duly obliged... but retaliated by kicking me out of the kitchen as the little Japanese Bobtail with the big Siberian Tiger appetite started metaphorically wolfing down my dinner.

I wandered into the lounge, where the human guest of honour seemed to be toying with her caipirinha and was just on the verge of picking up a huge, hardback book from the Sakamoto covered coffee table.

'Ah Nelson-san, your erudite and cosmopolitan owner (erudite and cosmopolitian??? **Owner???**) told me that he is fascinated by all things oriental, which makes a pleasant change from most of the gweilos I have ever come across. And he loves also Ryuichi Sakamoto-san. I have a feeling I may have finally met the one.'

(Imposter per écheance??)

As far as I was aware, his 'oriental fascination' extended to a dead Bonzai Plant and Chicken Chow Mein with fried rice and prawn crackers #34 from our local *Fu Kin Yu Sooluz Gweilo* Chinese Takeaway... I was going to say, before remembering his request to 'not cock it up for him and ruin the evening.'

Her eyes glanced back to the huge book. Uh oh, I know which book that is. I think the fawning imperial oaf had made (when he was feeling particularly 'erudite and cosmopolitan') a *faux pas*.

Before I could leap on to the table and spread myself over the book, she had picked it up, observing the emaciated bodies of Allied Prisoners of War in Burma, circa 1943, on the front cover.

*'Rats, Rice and Weevils.'* That is a most unusual book title. What is this book about?'

**'Japanese Home Cooking...'** I blurted out, with my newly-discovered, Ninja-like powers of deception. 'It is by the world-famous Okinawan Chef, Goro Ramenseki …'I continued, hoping she
would put it back down, *without opening it*, next to the newly purchased (and unopened) Book of Five Rings.

'But I wouldn't bother reading it, if I were you, as his recipes are terrible. Just look at the effect his food has had on his customers on that photo. I'm surprised they didn't sue him, let alone agree to appear on his book.'

'That is fair enough, I never rated Okinawan food either - or Korean, for that matter. '

'I'm afraid that I cannot venture an opinion, having never had Okinawan, Korean or, for that matter, Japanese cat food. But I expect raw tuna must be very popular?' I said, still trying to deflect her away from the book's real contents, with the mental dexterity required for an Aikido Black Belt Exam.

'But what a strange name for a cookery book…'

'It's the name of his new restaurant in Islington.'

*Phew, hopefully I can relax now and start to enjoy the evening.*

I flopped down and spread myself over his 12-disc box set of *'Armageddon in the Pacific - 1941-1945'*.
*'Uh, oh… she wants me to put a DVD on,'* I thought, as she moved towards me, rather stealthily.

She then, in hushed tones, confided in me:
'Nelson-san, what is the gweilo expression? Please do not make a scene out of this for me, but I do not wish to offend your lovely, kind owner (Excuse me? Who? Have I entered a parallel universe??) but I will have an allergic reaction to this drink if it contains limes. Generally, I hyperventilate and just need some oxygen – but, in extreme cases, I have to be rushed to hospital within 20 minutes - otherwise the allergic reaction could cause me to suffer a heart seizure.'
'WHAT???' I thought, with wide-eyed, Zen-less horror… assassinating the main guest of honour would have to come close to the zenith of *'cocking it up for me and ruining the evening'*…

'But I would dishonour your gracious owner (now hang on a minute…) if I did not at least have a mouthful of this drink, which he told me he had spent hours preparing with Barbadian sugar and organic limes that he had bought especially in my own honour… from Morocco.'

I thought about checking *Maurice and Sons* website to see if they had recently opened up a supermarket in Marrakesh, but then I realised she was about to sip Romeo's potion so...

**I HAD TO MAKE AN INSTANT DECISION** as she was about to place the glass to her lips with a Socratic mix of resignation and dignity. So I sprang at her like a coiled tiger, knocking it out of harm's way with a left hook (the jiu-jitsu lesson from Kiku had already reaped rewards) just as Emperor Ho Chi Minh the Mendacious strutted in.

Before I had time to explain, he yelled at me for spilling the drink on his brand new rug... at which point, Nene started sobbing, saying contritely, with head bowed…

'Please forgive me, I am so sorry. I am so ashamed of myself.'

This was definitely not a Zen moment for me as her apology actually made matters worse with Genghis Khan, now riding in full gallop across the Apoplectic Plains of Mercuria, accusing me of upsetting her - with his new found knowledge of Japanese anthropology.

'See how upset she is - you clumsy, braindead, in-bred oaf of a cat?

This latest, unwarranted barb made me bolt upright like a slighted samurai warrior.

I gave him a sideways look, as I unsheathed all my claws – but, unfortunately, they got stuck in his handmade Chinese Rug; I looked down to see that I was rooted to the spot. Despite my best efforts, I could not move one paw. However, the imperial fawning fool assumed that I was bowing my own head in shame.

The room was starting to resemble a field full of wilting sunflowers.

Ming the Merciless continued his rampaging tirade, but at least he didn't swear at me:

'Being of noble Japanese blood, Nene feels ashamed that she has ruined my rug - when it's all your fault for spilling her drink, you idiot. She is too polite to blame you. Do you have any idea where I had to buy those limes from?

'Well, now you ask…'

'Be silent you insolent, stupid, in-bred mog. You've already ruined the evening and we haven't even left the house yet… all I asked of you was to behave with some decorum and a modicum of respect… just this once. And - surprise, surprise - you do exactly the opposite. I wish I'd got myself a nice little Westie or an obedient little Beagle…

'A Beagle???'

'…You should apologise to her and…'

**'RICK-SAN, PLEASE STOP SHOUTING, YOU FOUL-TEMPERED DROP KICK.'** Piped up the previously demure Nene, leaving us both stunned.

The Mongol Warlord's rampaging charge came to a screeching halt.

186

*My sentiments entirely*, I thought gleefully, when I had recovered from the shock; feeling joyous and exonerated, in equal measure.

In the resultant tranquillity, a grasshopper could have heard a cherry blossom drop in a Zen Buddhist garden.

She then regained her composure: 'Your adorable and noble little cat probably just saved my life. You should be proud of him.' Explained the grateful Nene, before telling him about her medical condition.

The, by now, rather rotund looking Kiku poked her head round the door to see what was going on and instantly adopted a (Sumo-esque) fighting pose - indicating to me that, in the blink of an eye, she was ready to use her jiu-jitsu skills on him - if necessary. I was taking quite a shine to all things Japanese…

Though I was inwardly grinning like Lewis Carroll's Cheshire Cat (also a British Shorthair: Mr. Carroll had impeccable class), I kept an inscrutable visage (later described as 'smug and insolent' by DROP KICK-san) as espoused in The Book of Five Rings.

I did explain to Kiku afterwards, fearing she may assassinate him at midnight with a sharpened worming dispenser when I wasn't looking, that it was all a misunderstanding. I had damaged the very expensive Chinese rug soon after arrival – thinking that one of the dragons it depicted was real.

Plus… he wasn't a bad tyrant really, apart from trying to insist that he was Top Dog (as he called it) as he had paid for us to see Berwick Rangers the following weekend.

*DROP KICK-san does have a certain ring to it*, I thought to myself, as I carefully placed the *Japanese Cookery Book* under his Chinese rug.

This book had been a present from an ex-banking colleague and his wife from Sydney: Brad and Charlene Gontroppovski, who had turned their backs on the materialistic, greed-driven, corporate world, which they had grown to despise, and emigrated to the tropical paradise of Papua New Guinea.

'Why can't they send me something useful like an imitation *Sekonda* Watch? Or even a fake *Lacoste* Polo Shirt - even if one sleeve is four inches longer than the other and the dye runs out – ruining the rest of my washing?' Rick-san had once complained to me.

Having read a recent postcard sent from Vanuatu, I thought they seemed to be much more ecologically aware than him, as they dedicated much of their lives to snorkeling, sailing and jet skiing around the Pacific, saving scallops in the Ocean.

'Why can't he do something ecologically worthwhile like this or at least vacuum around my bean bag and clean out my litter tray more often (using eco-friendly cat litter)?' I mused.

Their next mission was to save the greatly endangered Screaming Red Bellied Mexican Jalapeno Munching Frog and set up a refuge for abandoned Chihuahuas (slightly less stupid than Beagles), suffering from eczema and various other skin disorders.

It did seem strange to me that Brad and Charlene, who dedicated so much time to saving God's lesser creatures and owned a pet Irish Setter (infinitely more stupid than Beagles), should boast about having eaten dog during a 10-day cruise along the Mekong River (to me eating a stuffed olive is risqué) so I hope for their Irish Setter's sake that it does not poop on their carpet.

Having sat amongst the Barmy Army in a Test Match at the SCG (dropping out of the corporate banking world necessitated buying the cheapest tickets) they had contemptuously informed Rick-san that '…the English are the most vile, racist, unsophisticated and uncivilised bunch of drongoes they have ever had the misfortune to sit next to for 4 days.'

'Have they never watched *'Talentless and Deluded'* or the 13-part documentary *'Boozed Up Brits In Ayia Napa'*?' I asked my equally bewildered LHC.

I did not know whether they included British Blues in that group, but I've always got on quite well with Chartreux, Burmese, Abyssinians, Maine Coons and Spotted Mists: I must admit, however, that I have never been overly keen on Siamese… they just never shut up. But what do you expect from a foreign cat?

He felt that he should suggest that they were over-generalising, but trying to convince them to see someone else's point of view was futile.

So… I decided to launch a defence on his behalf by writing and diplomatically suggesting that it is a bit unfair to label the entire population of Britain as racist when Tikka Masala is the national dish:

'…even I like it and I am a cat, though I need three litter trays the next day if I have eaten Lamb

Hyderabadi. The British must be a very friendly breed - as it seems that everyone from Eastern Europe has emigrated here. You will be pleased to know that since you emigrated, England has become a much more civilised place to live in, although, due to the recent furore over horsemeat, it will be some years before the British adopt the civilised practise of eating dog.

Meanwhile, the more liberal members of the Coalition Government are hoping to re-introduce public hangings, prison hulk ships on the Thames, debtors jails, fox hunting, cock fighting, public flogging, hard labour in prisons and tormenting the inmates in mental institutions by tickling their feet with feathers. It will be Bedlam.

Must go... I have to put out the burning cross that's on my front lawn.

Aplogies for sany speling errorz it is verry hard seeing teh keyboard through teh little eye slits in my white hood.'

Four months later, Rick the Drongo told me he was surprised that the Gontroppovskis still had not replied and he blamed me for upsetting them. But I had a feeling we may never hear from them again after they told us in their last letter that they had been invited - by their friendly, tubby neighbours - as special guests of honour, to a traditional Port Morseby Long Pig BBQ.

**The Opera Itself**

On the way to the King Harold Opera House I had a brainwave: 'This episode has inspired me to sit down and draft my own version of The Art of War, later on in the year... after having completed my diary.'

As we took our seats in the box, Nene apologised for her outburst - blaming it on her nature as she came from a warlike Samurai family and said she merely meant to address him as 'a foul-mouthed half-wit - not a DROP KICK'.

For some reason, this didn't seem to reassure Rick-san - who very quickly reciprocated her apology and then - knock me down with an origami crane - he apologised to me.

Or was this merely an act of reciprocated sarcasm? A dose of my own flea powder?

This must have been more excruciatingly painful for him than the death of a thousand cuts.

Then I thought... *has he booked me in for a special appointment at the vets in the morning*?

I had also been worried about being compelled to wear my Rod Stewart tartan cat collar, but was delighted to learn that I'd been bought a dickie bow cat collar especially for the occasion - so I cockily sauntered past the open-shirted, jean-clad plebeians and their 'fur coat and no knickers' partners (to quote the snooty, operatic cat abuser: perhaps it was their mating season?). I felt like a feline Beau Brummel.

I was as proud as punch, as Kiku (the cute little Bobtail), had also agreed to come along.

Having finally regained his composure and sense of self-importance, Rick-san told me that I was under the strictest orders to behave appropriately and not put a paw out of line:

'Please try not to ruin anything, steal anyone's salmon canapés in the interval, complain about the quality of the milk, generally upset anyone, complain you're bored half-way through, or worst of all, fall asleep during the performance. These tickets cost me an absolute fortune.'

The Divine One of little faith.

So, with the reverence I would only reserve for the Emperor... (if I ever should meet him, upon a visit to the Tokyo Imperial Palace) I bowed loyally and obsequiously.

The Emperor of Yorkshire was not impressed: 'And you can cut out that smart**** attitude too. And above all, don't start howling with emotion at the end - like you did after *Skyfall.*'

'Rick-san, it's just a simple love story isn't it? I hardly think that Madama Butterfly is going to do something ridiculous like disembowel herself in the final scene. After all, that didn't happen in The Magic Flute.'

Rick-san's response was to shake his head and mutter that he should have left me at home in the kitchen.

About 64 bar staff in black suits and white dickie bows turned up and took their places in the orchestra pit. I thought: '*...the management of this* *place certainly get a pound of flesh out of their staff. I bet they only pay them the minimum wage… but times are tough and I suppose employees of any company just have to be grateful they've got a job - unless they are the beleaguered Chief Executive of the Scotty Bingo Bank of Jacobites.*

Nene and Kiku seemed very excited, whilst we had no idea what to expect, but we were told that it was a haunting love story set in Japan, circa 1900.

Puccini-san and I had never been to an opera before and we had a box close to the stage - so we didn't have to mix with the riff-raff in the cheap seats below, who were undoubtedly low-class moggies - as none of them wore dickie bows. This seemed much better than the garlic concert at Celtic Connections, but my heart sank when I was told it would be sung in *Italian*. I was relying on Kiku to translate the performance from Japanese to English for me.

'Aren't there any talented opera singers in Britain? Surely there must be at least one mezzo-soprano between Cindy Carcrash and Ladettes Yodelling?' I asked with a sense of resignation, hoping that we were at least to be spared any opera singers who would inadvertently bring with them 200,000 still-enraged Parisians: demanding that everyone stand up in the theatre and sing *La Marseillaise* during Act 1 Scene 1 again, during the drinks interval and finally at the end.

I looked through Nene's miniature binoculars and scanned the horizon, and I simply could not see

Wiggo anywhere in the audience - which was a promising sign.

What I did see was a garish paint job on the ceiling - only my penitential cousin Winston and his equally spliffed out human companion could have done that.

Rick-san sat in the box as proud as Puccini, saying how nice it was to enjoy a civilised evening with urbane and sophisticated company - rather than being stood like a sardine with the drunken rabble in bars like *Morehopethanjoys* until 4 a.m.

'Thank you, that feeling is partially reciprocated,' I said, bashfully.

'I didn't mean you,' he replied, clearly having regained his sense of humour.

The opera duly started. I was hoping that it might be a comedy, after the unfortunate incident with the caipirinhas.

Nene started sobbing, saying that it made her homesick. I pounced on this opportunity to say that we could make her feel happier by going to a Teppanyaki Restaurant after the performance - but Rick-san's parsimony had returned like a divine wind.

The music was very pleasant and the orchestra seemed very good, which could be largely explained by the fact that *Quid Pro Quo* were not there to play a heavy metal rendition of '*See them! They're climbing the summit of the hill!* ' - plus we had a nice view of the stage from our box.

In Act I, Pinkerton marries the young geisha, signing a 999-year marriage contract - which gave both Rick-san and two thirds of the male members of the audience heart palpitations. After the wedding ceremony, her Uncle burst in, cursing her for renouncing her Buddhist religion. She must have become a Protestant - so I would have been annoyed too.

In Act II, Pinkerton had disappeared; probably been posted to Haiti. The new Rangers supporter has the chance to marry a wealthy Japanese Prince, but rejects him, in the hope that Lieutenant Pinkerton will return one fine day. If I had been *Suzuki* I would have suggested that she should take her chances on a Nagasaki Internet dating site.

It seemed quite a nice love story and I particularly liked the humming chorus.

In Act III, Pinkerton - whose Christian name should have been Winston - returns to Japan with his new American wife. '*He must be a Mormon,*' I surmised.

It was during Act III, however, that this fine opera threatened to come to an abrupt end. Alone on stage, the geisha reveals a huge knife and prepares to kill herself; I thought, '*…her singing isn't that bad – surely?*'

Perching on the edge of the box, I looked around and was absolutely disgusted that no-one in the audience - and this was supposedly the cream of Yorkshire society - was going to do anything about it: they all just sat there staring.

*These people are no better than their ancestors who used to watch public executions.*

The bounder Pinkerton was nowhere to be seen, which is typical. *Probably because Nagasaki harbour has no oil reserves, otherwise he would have come back, along with the entire US Northern Pacific Fleet and the Asia-Pacific Business Development Senior Deputy Vice-Presidents of CRAPPC, Friedbullsass del Rey, Colonel Lightbulb and Louisiana Frazzled Capons*, I mused, disdainfully.

She must be a manic-depressive and desperately needs psychiatric counselling, as it was only an hour ago that she was singing about it being *One Fine Day*.

Nene and Kiku were both bawling their eyes out, whilst Rick-san was snoring lightly - having nodded off in Act II.

Similar to the caipirinha incident of two hours earlier, I had to make a split-second decision as neither Nene nor Kiku were in a fit state to intervene. The distraught leading lady picked up the knife and started singing again.

*If anything, I think her voice is actually getting better - but these prima donnas do have a reputation for being neurotic and hard on themselves. It's now or never. If no-one is going to do anything about it, then I will have to act, in order to rescue her from spilling her guts.*

I mounted the rail on our box and estimated that if I could build enough momentum by wriggling my frelon/ Good Looooordy-scarred hindquarters - like a turbo-charged *Kenwood* Food Processor - then I should be able to propel myself onto the stage and grab her knife, before she does herself a mischief.

As I went flying through the air like one of Wagner's Valkyries (admittedly not the most apt of analogies, in the circumstances) I implored to her as loudly as I could:

'Don't do it, Coco Pop. He's not worth it. You've got your whole life ahead of you. There are lots of other fishes in the Pacific and you can always get work singing in a jazz club.'

Unfortunately, I misjudged the distance and entered a downward spiral (resembling a Stuka Bomber with its Jericho-Trumpet siren wailing) - diving towards my unintended target, which happened to be a retired headmistress sitting in Row C Seat 27.

A few instants before I crash-landed on her head, she looked up and screamed:

'AAAAAAAAAAAAARRRRRRRRHHHHH, it's a flying fox. They've all got ra…'

Her screams were muffled when I landed on her face, knocking her unconscious.

As I rolled onto her ample lap, I managed to look up and see that Coco Pop had dropped the knife and was staring at me with her mouth agape - which I assumed to be eternal gratitude.

*Probably some kind of Post-Traumatic Stress Syndrome, having realised, with hindsight, what irrevocable harm she was about to impose on herself...* I surmised.

I then noticed that she had been joined by Suzuki, Goro, Sharpless and the heartless cad Pinko - who looked incandescent with rage. He stood there shaking uncontrollably (racked with guilt, I imagine). With his white, Naval uniform and bright red face he looked like a Belisha Beacon.

The retired headmistress woke up to see me looking at her and I was about to apologise and explain my noble intentions - when she started screaming again. The poor woman was delirious, probably due to too many gin & tonics during the interval. Then she started shouting:

'Get that ******* flying fox off me, it'll ******* have rabies.'

Which I thought was language most unbecoming for someone in her line of work, plus her grammar left much to be desired - not placing an adjective, no matter how coarse, immediately before a noun. No wonder there are so many illiterate, teenage delinquents on the dole...

I was about to give her a piece of my mind, in this regard, when an unsophisticated ruffian threw his opera glasses at me.

Using my feline reflexes, I ducked, and they instead hit the occupant of Row B Seat 25 - knocking him into the occupant of Row A Seat 25.

I was beginning to understand the bizarre human concept called the domino effect.

The occupant of Row A Seat 25 took exception to being head butted in the salubrious surroundings of the King Harold Opera House, so promptly turned round and punched the chap behind him, who had, up to this point, been having a relaxing evening with his wife... after they had decided to give their rocky marriage a second chance instead of taking the long, twisting path to the barren wasteland called 'divorce'.

I tried to tell him: 'I know from Grasshopper's experience that if it doesn't work out the first time then, believe you me, it won't get any better the second time round. You should have just agreed to split everything 50:50 and get on with the rest of your lives...'

To which his peroxided wife responded by saying: 'Mind your own \*\*\*\*\*\*\* business. I'm a Legal Secretary so I know EXACTLY where I stand with my rights in the family law court.'

Then she belted the occupant of Row C Seat 26 with her handbag so hard that he flew into Row F.

By now, all of the women in Rows A to G, Seats 20-34 had started screaming, as though they were auditioning for the humming chorus (...sung by the witches in *Macb... err... The Scottish Play, I have to call it, for fear of supernatural reprisals*).

There was now pandemonium everywhere. Most of the audience were standing up and shouting abuse (I did notice their previously suave voices now carried distinctive Yorkshire accents, which is what often happens when one's inhibitions are cast aside, so it must do them good to escape the straitjacket of society's expectations and get it all off their chests at these operatic performances.)

Men and women were getting into fisticuffs with one another, and there were calls for money to be refunded - a bit rich, bearing in mind the performance had almost finished.

Typical Yorkshire folk, I sighed, shaking my head knowingly, always trying to get 'owt fer nowt' (I think that's the expression).

I have to say that they were generally acting like an ill-mannered rabble, more suited to watching *The Beggar's Opera* than the serene *Madama Butterfly*.

The entire orchestra had ceased playing and were standing up to witness the scene unfolding in front of them.

I managed to run the gauntlet of opera glasses, handbags, telescopic umbrellas and stiletto heels - and one pair of dentures - to reach the stage, checking on Coco Pop, who was sitting on the side of the stage, weeping about this being her first night, which I thought was a bit ungrateful as had it not been for me it would have also been her last night.

'Must be overcome with emotion, poor lass. Being a manic-depressive, it probably doesn't take much to send her toppling over the edge…' I empathised, then I saw the black-hearted Lt. Belisha Beacon steaming directly towards me, like a U.S. Navy Destroyer under orders of *'Damn the torpedoes, full steam ahead'*, with most of the steam coming out of his ears.

**'DO YOU KNOW WHAT YOU HAVE DONE? YOU HAVE RUINED MY ENTIRE CAREER.'**

**'YOU'RE NOT GOOD ENOUGH TO BE AN ADMIRAL,'** I replied, giving him a verbal slap in the chops with disgust and contempt, even though I had to admit that Lord Nelson was also of the philandering type (must be a trait in Naval Officers).

'If I get my hands on you, I'll wring your…' at this point, a French Horn player stood up and shouted…

'Yeah, I think you're rubbish too. You're always late for rehearsals and you always sing out of key. You've got a worse voice than Long John Silver's parrot. You should buzz off back to Middlesbrough.'

I must admit that I never knew about there being a U.S. Naval base in Teesside. It must be top secret, so that indiscrete horn player should stop blowing his own trumpet - as there might be Cuban spies in the audience.

Most of the audience had been baying for my blood (clearly disappointed that I prevented the public exhibition of hara kiri.) And then, I suddenly started to receive my own humming chorus of cheers: 'We're with the cat. We think you're rubbish too.'

'Go the cat. Brilliant acrobatics. Best night's entertainment I've had in years…' which was accompanied by more cheering and clapping.

'This is my first time. I'm coming back next week. And I'd always thought opera was boring.'

'Far better than wasting an entire afternoon watching Leeds United lose 1-0 and half the cost too.' Which led to the biggest cheer of the entire evening.

'It's my first time as well. This is more fun than hang gliding. I'm getting a season ticket.'

'It should be you committing hara kiri - you talentless apology for a Lieutenant.'

Thinking '…*I wouldn't want to get an Annual Performance Appraisal like that,*' I looked behind me to castigate his Commanding Officer, as he should know better than anyone else that this practise contravened Naval Regulations but I could not spot him in the audience (must be off duty and in civvies).

Then I saw Kiku jumping up and down in the box, punching her paw in the air shouting: 'Allez Allez Allez Nelson.' Knowing I had won her over, I felt as proud as punch: *…she can speak French too. Is there no end to her talents*?

The occupant of Row A Seat 25, looking a bit bloodied and dishevelled, groggily got to his feet to tell everyone that he had not paid £78 for the privilege of being assaulted, he was a District Judge and that The Housecarl Opera Company hadn't heard the end of this. I thought this was most generous of him, as this fine opera company could do with any free publicity it could get in these cash-strapped, cost-cutting, bourgeois times.

Pinkerton had a heated exchange with the entire brass section, until a tuba was shoved over his head, then five security guards came running towards me like Valkyries on steroids. I decided I was capable of making my own way to Valhalla and, spotting a neon sign stating Emergency Exit, sidestepped each of the brutes with the deftness of a Stade Français winger.

One half of the audience was screaming abuse at me - whilst the other half were cheering me to the rafters. I felt like I was being substituted with two minutes to go at Parkhead, having scored the winning goal for Celtic in a Glasgow Derby. (Shunsuke Nakamura had laid on an inch-perfect pass to my front paws, having returned especially from Japan).

With a friendly wave of my paw to the Royal Box (where one Philistine had managed to sleep through the whole of the improvised final scene)... I departed.

I decided that it might be wise not to even venture near my cat flap for 72 hours but, to my amazement, when I returned, I was in the good books of the Emperor.

Hmm, there must be an ulterior motive for this, as I don't ever remember him being remotely pleased to see me before.

It transpired that Nene thought I was such a noble and gallant cat that, had I been a Japanese Blue, I would have been a worthy member of a Samurai household.

She had decided that this reflected well on him too - and the way *he had brought me up.*

As such, she regarded him as being a true English Gentleman, kind to boot, though a little volatile for a Samurai.

I thanked Dr. Dolittle for everything he had done for me, in particular, cancelling my insurance cover. I also attributed her abysmal powers of judgment down to the lingering effect of the caipirinha fumes.

Kiku just keeps purring at the mention of my name - proving that she clearly possesses far superior powers of judgment. Plus, I had mentioned our trip to Berwick… saving him that awkward conversation.

**Belated Christmas Greetings from Norway**

On the 31$^{st}$ I received a belated Christmas Card signed by Dr. Bunsenbernassen, Ms. Kuulsen and Fenrik Trollengaard who all sent me their fondest regards & best wishes for 2013 and said I would be welcome back in Norway at any time.

Fenrik Trollengaard said that morale in his platoon had collapsed since they lost their immensely popular mascot, he was particularly concerned about the mental state of Korporal Knut Appissen, and the entire platoon's first aid skills had regressed.

Sersjant Jokkum Cheeruppen's attempt to boost morale by placing a stuffed otter in the Junior Ranks' Bar had only made matters worse. Korporal Appisen, the Other Ranks' Social Club Treasurer, was utterly inconsolable when he audited the accounts and found that kr3500 of the kr4125 set aside for the platoon's Christmas Party had been used by Sersjant Cheeruppen to purchase the surrogate mascot from *Henriksen & Lund Taxidermists* in Oslo's Old Town.

At his court martial, the quixotic Sersjant Cheeruppen defended his actions stating that he had to contribute kr499 from his own salary to buy the much-maligned otter and that he and Herr Henriksen agreed that it bore a far closer resemblance to myself then the other stuffed options available viz. an elk with a missing antler, a wild boar's head on a plinth, a dozen red squirrels in various, gymnastic poses and a rampant Siberian Tiger. He was reprimanded for insubordination for adding that the stuffed Siberian Tiger was so expensive that only an Orlogskaptein on a Naval Attorney's salary could afford the kr48,000 asking price.

Happily, Sersjant Cheeruppen was exonerated as it was Christmas Eve and the Judge Advocate accepted Fenrik Trollengaard's testimony that, having lost the popular Erik the Cat last winter during an Arctic Survival Exercise then losing the even more popular Nelssen (meg), morale was low enough in his platoon without his men now losing their highly-regarded and kind-hearted Sersjant.

So the inanimate otter was swiftly moved to the Sersjants' Mess whilst the Officers' Mess acquired a rampant Siberian Tiger. The tiger was paid for by the well-heeled Battalion Adjutant Kaptein Mooseknobbeler whose Uncle Rolf (a retired optometrist and Reservist Oberst), it was rumoured, had mistaken Erik for a scavenging Arctic Fox whilst hunting for elk during the survival exercise.

They all lamented that I had been unable to be with the platoon and the staff from the University's School of Astrophysics on New Year's Eve at their joint party at a jazzy new bar in Oslo called 'The

Screaming Tomcat' which specialised in vodka cocktails.

Dr Bunsenbernassen particularly liked the *'Mach 1.8 Blue Bomber'* (25ml Stolichnaya Gold Vodka, 40ml Blue Curacao, 15ml Linie Aquavit, 100ml of soda water, four ice cubes and a quartered lime) which the genial bar owner claimed, seemingly with a whiff of sarcasm, could fuel a MiG-29 Fighter even one 1,200 kilometres off course...

He also liked the *'Hallucinating Flying Cossack'* (equal 25ml measures of Navigator Vodka and Apal Hardanger Eplebrennevin plus 75ml of cloudy apple juice, served with crushed ice and a sprig of mint).

Towards midnight, an exasperated Ms. Kuulsen demanded that the bar's resident Scarlet Macaw, *Icarussky*, be ejected from the bar for continually wolf-whistling at her.

Just after 1.00am, having downed a dozen *'Stormin' Normans'* (the French equivalent of the 'Hallucinating Flying Cossack' – see recipe below), the poker-faced Korporal Appisen climbed onto the small stage and delivered an impromptu stand-up comedy routine which had everyone weeping uncontrollably with mirth. The bar owner was so impressed that he made him three complimentary new cocktails: *'On the flight path to nowhere'*, *'Yep, we're lost'* and a *'Nordic Riga'*.

After drinking his ninth cocktail, all Dr. Bunsenbernassen could remember before collapsing was a worse for wear Fenrik Trollengaard ordering his men to shoot a moose's head hanging over the bar, which *he insisted* had insulted his wife, before being escorted out of the bar by Konstabel Gunnar Kufussen of the Naval Military Police.

A great Nordic night was had by all.

*'Stormin' Norman' =*
equal 25ml measures of Grey Goose Vodka and Calvados plus 75ml of French apple juice (ideally from Neufchâtel-en-Bray), served with crushed ice and a sprig of mint.

# February

**Female Mackems and the Border Clash**

We popped up for a weekend to see Berwick Rangers play the once mighty Glasgow Rangers and got there via Sunderland, the breeding ground of Mackems and possibly the coldest place in the British Isles.

We stayed with an old mate of my LHC and had a civilised evening on the Friday (enjoying a rump steak dinner in *The Lambton Worm*).

Despite the fact that it was cold enough for a polar bear to get hypothermia, the pub was full of scantily clad women. My LHC's Mackem mate said that he felt overdressed (he had on a long-sleeved shirt). Are these Mackems mad? It was freezing.

I'd thought I'd seen it all in Ribald-upon-Trent, a small market town where everyone seemed to be inter-related (human for inter-bred), but when we walked into the pub for dinner, I almost shot out backwards. It was full of obese, furless, old women caked in mascara, wearing stockings, suspenders & high heels, with very deep voices, painted arms and hairy chests, downing one pint after another - as though they were joining the Quakers the next day.

I had never seen any women like this before, not even on his scary Internet dating site.

The gargoyles on Notre Dâme Cathedral were more attractive.

Each gargoyle woman seemed to be accompanied by a slightly less grotesque woman in more normal clothing, but caked in even more make-up, plus peroxided hair. They kept addressing each other as *'pet'.*

These had to be the scariest pets I'd ever seen - other than a komodo dragon.

I always thought that the North-East was a bit old-fashioned in its attitudes to same sex relationships (must admit, so are felines, though we're grateful if we've still got all our reproductive organs intact). I assumed the peroxided ones with the heavily painted faces (perhaps there was a clown convention in town?) were, and I believe the human term is, lipstick lesbians?

If this is what all of the women in Sunderland look like when they are dressed up to the nines, then Sunderland would have to be the gay capital of Europe.

When I mentioned this to my LHC's Mackem pal, he said he didn't find it very funny (I was being serious) and he said if I said anything like that again, he would make me stand on my own amongst the 3,000 hard-core Rangers supporters at the Berwick game the next day.

Gulp. I'd heard about the razor gangs in Glasgow and had visions of being lynched as the half-time entertainment. That made me apologise instantly, even though I didn't know what I had done wrong, and I kept my head down for the rest of the evening – but I had truthfully never seen so many weird looking women in my life.

I had hoped to see the local Mackem team, as apparently they are called 'The Black Cats'. With a nickname like that they must have some good goalkeepers - though if they are felines of a similar size to myself, it seems most unreasonable to expect them to defend a goal which is 8-feet by 24-feet in size.

Are they panthers, perhaps?

I'd also been told the current Manager used to manage the Bhoys a few years ago, so it would be nice to see him again ( being a loyal Celtic supporter) and tell him how I intended to support Berwick and maybe sing the odd Celtic song in his honour… as the 'Gers fans would be a safe distance away.

The next morning, we set off through the snow to Berwick and, driving up the A1, we passed through some very picturesque scenery. His Mackem pal said there was a beautiful, old monastery in the sea. I didn't realise there had ever been any seafaring monks. I asked if they were from the Order of Neptune, which I thought was quite witty, but he just glared at me.

With his threat of the previous evening still ringing in my ears, I cast my eyes seawards, towards the monastery and I have to say that it looked nothing special to me: just a hut on a knoll - surrounded by water.

It could have been Alcatraz, as far as I was concerned.

He then went on to say that 1,200 years ago, the monks were forever being slaughtered; the monastery looted by Viking raiders.

I should have known better, but I asked why they didn't fight back and invest in some decent 5-lever mortice locks from *IKEA* (admittedly a Viking retailer). Luckily, he was driving, so was limited in what he could physically do to me, but he replied - with his face getting redder than a Berserker – that the monks were simple, sandal-wearing men of peace who played the harp, meditated, wove tapestries and prayed all day.

*Death would have been a merciful release*, I mused, thinking I would rather have been a Viking; they seemed to be much more fun.

So... why didn't the monks learn to defend themselves? They could have sent for a monk from China to teach them Kung Fu.

Fearing this banter was going beyond the pale, my LHC interjected and asked what we thought the score would be - assuming the game had not been called off.

They predicted scores of 0-7 and 0-10 to Rangers and then '…as a laugh, let's ask your stupid cat for his expert opinion…'

I chose to ignore this blunt-edged barb of sarcasm and suggested 3-1 to Rangers, with Berwick taking a $6^{th}$ minute lead - compliments of an own goal. Rangers equalising *with a penalty*, 3 minutes later - before taking a 2-1 lead in the last minute of the first half and eventually winning 3-1... compliments of a 66th minute goal.

There was silence for 2 minutes, before my LHC desperately fumbled for a *William Safeashouses* betting app on his new smartphone. His hands were going like bees' wings (something else the monks made for the Vikings) as he had only 15 minutes remaining to master his new toy and submit *'his'* bet and *he* got odds of 45-1 for *my* exact prediction.

'If we both put £1 on and we win this, it will pay for dinner and all our beer in Berwick!!' he said, bouncing up and down with excitement on his seat like a modern-day Viking about to disembark in choppy waters at Holy Island.

However, just as he was about to place the bet, he lost the signal. This led to so many oaths and profanities being shouted at his *smartphone*, especially concerning *Sonearly*, that I am surprised it didn't have Thor scurrying for cover behind Ericsson. Then, 13 minutes later, calm was restored - along with the mobile signal.

'Hey Nelson, I've got to re-input every detail. Right, give me your exact prediction again. **Quick. Come on, chop chop.'**

To which I replied, still smarting from the insult of 16 minutes earlier and not being asked politely: 'Being a stupid cat, with the memory of a goldfish... regretfully, I cannot remember,' then I gazed admiringly out of the car's rear window at the huge stone mansions on the outskirts of Berwick.

We checked into a quaint little B&B called The White Swan (alas not on the menu) before setting off to the Maracana of Scottish Borders, as described by the Mackem pal.

By now, I was in the bad books of both my human companions and was given a 'Scarborough Warning' - even though I estimated that to be about 150 miles due south. In the circumstances I chose not to mention this geographical inaccuracy, and I was sternly told that: '…if you make any more **impudent, disrespectful or smarta\*\*\* quips** then I'll lock you in the bedroom for the rest of the day - without a litter tray! Just remember who's the boss around here.'

'Does that mean, Skipper, that I will be confined to the metaphorical doghouse?' I couldn't help asking El Supremo.  At which point, he marched off, muttering to himself that he should have never given in to his wife; he always wanted a Westie, not a cat.

Charming…

Berwick-upon-Tweed itself is a very nice, historical town but the humans are a bit strange.

Everyone talks with a broad Scots accent, all the pubs serve Scottish Beer, they eat porridge and haggis for breakfast and their team plays in the Scottish Third Division. Plus the local infantry regiment, the King's Own Scottish Borderers, wore tartan trews so I not unreasonably assumed that all its residents were indeed Scottish.

On the way to the game, Bligh, Mackem and I stopped in at the local *Asda* supermarket. The Team Captain and his Mackem No 2 had gone off to '…stock up on provisions for the game', so I was busy admiring the humans' chocolate biscuits when a frail old lady, who must have been 85 if she was a day (I think that's the expression), screeched to a sudden halt in her mobility scooter, next to me.

She looked distressed, forlorn and helpless as she had dropped her gloves on the floor and was unable to retrieve them. So she asked whether anyone would be kind enough to pick up her 'wee gluvvies' as she had terrible problems with arthritis, and she was scared that her scooter would topple over, breaking her hip and she could not afford to pay for a hip replacement.

Other than two shoplifting Rangers fans, there were no humans around, so, being the gallant gent that I am, I duly obliged, deciding that I would politely decline any reward that she may proffer.

With an old, arthritic hand, she gently stroked my neck, whilst complimenting me on my kind act, which made me feel for the plight of this lovely old lady even more - but I managed, with the stoicism for which British Shorthairs are justly renowned, to hold back my tears.

As Skip and Mackem were getting reacquainted with their old mates Sam Smith, Art Guinness and Josh Tetley, I took the opportunity to while away some minutes by engaging in some pleasantries with this dear old lady about her charming and picturesque home town of Berwick: a bit like Whitby… but without any moggies.

She told me that she had lived all her life in Berwick - save three years spent in Plymouth when her husband was in the Royal Marines - which was not much to her liking. She went on to say that her one regret in life was not emigrating to Australia in 1978, but, unfortunately, her husband (who was half-Dutch) was barred, due to his arrest after a drunken brawl in Portsmouth with three merchant sailors from Argentina, following the World Cup Final of that year.

She then went on to say that they had been happily married for 56 years, and once had a huge and ferocious Doberman - which her husband named Claudio Gentile - though she never understood why.

Unfortunately, her husband had died four years ago and life since then had been a constant struggle – as she was trying to live on a widow's Navy Pension. Even in Berwick, property prices had soared and it was hard keeping on top of her bills.

All the while she kept trying to insist on buying me a tin of cat food as a token of her gratitude (*Cat Master Chef*... not cheap rubbish, I hasten to add) but I nobly declined her kind offer, saying that, in these hard, triple-dip recessionary times, it was of paramount importance that she kept her hard-earned pension money for herself.

She told me that it was an absolute pleasure to have met me and if this country's penny-pinching and budget-blitzing Government Ministers were more like me, then Great Britain would indeed still be *Great* and lonely, old pensioners like herself would not be living on the breadline.

She lamented that she now had to leave *'...maa wee furry knight in shining armour'* to buy some porridge oats, a bottle of *Laphraiog Malt Whisky* and some *Highland Spring* Mineral Water, adding that she would always fondly remember my wee act of kindness.

Quixotically, I replied that the pleasure was all mine, and purred at how smitten I was with her lovely, soft, lilting Scottish accent - whilst gently rubbing my chin against her, as a valedictory sign of affection.

Her valedictory response was not quite what I expected...

She grabbed me by the throat in a vice-like grip and told me that her family had been fighting off the Scottish hordes since Flodden in 1513. The only good thing about Scotland was malt whisky and if I ever insulted her again by calling her SCOTTISH she would '**RIP MAA ******* HEAD OFF (laddie)'.**

She continued to rant & rave that she never did care for Taggart, Bill Shankly, Alex Salmond or the Bay City Rollers, her favourite subject at school was history, in particular the Battle of Culloden, she particularly resented Forfar Athletic for ejecting her from Station Park in 1986 for her alleged use of *'foul and abusive language'*, ditto Brechin City in 1998 and Albion Rovers in 2005. She felt she had been victimised by the Scots over many years simply for being English as she had been banned for 5 years by Stenhousemuir in 1993 for *'threatening behaviour'*; banned for 10 years by Stirling Albion in 2001 for running over a steward in her mobility scooter and banned for life by Alloa Athletic in 2008 for assaulting the Alloa Team Mascot with her thermos flask. If she had her way, the entire membership of the Scottish National Party would be banished to the Outer Hebrides and the only bit she liked about Mel Gibson's film *Braveheart*, was the execution scene at the end, which she found highly entertaining, adding that she was not overly fond of Australians either.

And finally, with a tear in her bloodshot eye, she lamented that she did not have much time left on this earth so her greatest fear in the after-life would be having to listen to 'Amazing Grace' being played on the bagpipes in perpetuity.

I declined to ask, mainly on account of being unable to breathe, why she had two packets of *Paterson's Shortbread,* a multipack of *Tunnoch's Caramel Wafers, a jar of Mackay's Dundee Orange Marmalade* and 300 grams of Aberdeen Angus Steak in her shopping basket and decided not to engage in any other small talk viz. whether she wanted Berwick Rangers or Glasgow Rangers to win that afternoon.

I was just grateful that her mobility scooter didn't have scythes attached to the wheels.

She finally let go, then rode off down the Bakery Aisle like a geriatric Hell's Angel stuck in first gear on Route 66 - whilst I lay on the floor by the *McVities Biscuits* sub-section, on my back with all four legs stretched out, gasping for breath - feeling like I was about to be spread-eagled by a Norse war party.

The unsympathetic Bligh and Coxswain, his Mackem pal, strolled around the corner, having loaded up on *Bounty Bars* and *Fruit Pastilles:* 'Let's get these as the cat doesn't like them...' I overheard Skip whisper.

*Here comes the Cavalry*, I mused, or more precisely Custer's reinforcements.

However, they berated me for choking on a *McVitie's Biscuit,* which they said I had purloined from a squashed packet that I had landed on half-strangled.

'Serves you right for stealing. And if the checkout girl charges me for that damaged packet of biscuits then it's coming out of your food allowance.'

Thank you...

I'd had quite enough of the North-East for one weekend. I didn't come to Berwick to be throttled, run over by a mobility scooter, insulted and then starved. I am not William Wallace. This is the last time I will ever visit Berwick.

Perhaps I could now just relax, forget about this unsavoury incident and enjoy the football match? At that thought, the octogenarian Boadicea/Lewis Hamilton/Berwick Comancheros mutant went whizzing past shouting: 'Stick it tae 'em at the game, bonnie laddies. The Police ull back yer up. We've spent 500 years keeping them Scotch booggas oot o' Berwick, ann we dinnae wanna see 'em 'ere agin.'

You don't get this at rugby.

**Berwick Rangers vs. Rangers**

As we walked out of the *Asda* store and through its car park, I was struck by how many cars had Glaswegian number plates. *Asda* must indeed be a fine supermarket if they are prepared to come all the way to Berwick for their weekly shopping. I half-expected to see an enraged, Nazi helmet adorned octogenarian ramming her mobility scooter, kamikaze style, into such cars.

We arrived at Berwick Rangers' stadium and I casually asked whether the Vikings had been the week before - judging by its condition, for which I received a cuff across my brow from Bligh.

Mackem had wisely bought us 3 tickets to sit in the Main Stand with the Home Supporters, as he knew that, being Roman Catholics, we were both ardent Celtic supporters... even though, being Protestant, he followed the Gers.

I was under strict orders, under pain of neutering, re-attachment, then re-neutering... not to wear my green, white and gold Celtic scarf or bobble hat, which I subserviently agreed to go along with.

'That makes a welcome change for you.. actually doing something I ask of you. **Are you ill?**'

Was Bligh's retort, which I thought was a trifle uncalled for. I refused to be drawn into a catty exchange by this snide comment - common in autocrats - but courteously thanked him for his concern about my welfare, adding: 'No, as far as I am aware, I have neither cat flu nor rabies, but be rest assured, you will be the first human to find out - if I ever get the latter.'

I was able to peer into the stadium as we were waiting to be searched by the hundreds of policemen barring the gate. It was like a sea of hi-viz yellow, which illuminated an otherwise dreary afternoon. I have to say that it was the most feline-friendly venue I had ever been to: there was a huge litter tray encircling the entire pitch, which was very considerate of them, but personally I would have preferred slightly more privacy whilst performing my ablutions - especially as the game was to be televised live.

I thought Berwick played in black and gold, so was surprised that all of the supporters going through our entrance were all wearing blue. Perhaps they had changed their kit for this season and lamented that - presumably having played in black and gold since 1884 - this was another proud old club that had thrown its heritage out of the ground. Maybe they had been taken over by a rich, Malaysian property tycoon, though looking on the bright side, they may now be selling Satay Chicken with rice - instead of pie and chips, during the half-time break.

As we entered the ground, having assured a suspicious steward that the *Bounty Bars* were to be used for nourishment, not missiles, we read a sign stating: 'Away Supporters'. I could not believe it. Being in their bad books, and having a throbbing pain in my brow, I was obsequiously relying on Marco Polo and Vasco da Gama to choose the correct entrance - of which there were but two. Yet despite these highly favourable 50:50 odds, they succeeded in wandering into the wrong entrance - from which there was no turning back, as the aforementioned steward said '… no-one in the away end was allowed to go into the home end'. My worst nightmare was about to be realised: spending 2 hours in the company of 3,000 of Rangers most die-hard, rabidly papist-hating, loyalist supporters.

We found space at the front of the stand, as far away as possible from the screaming hordes of Gers supporters… approximately six feet away. Despite the bitterly cold weather, I was taken aback by the Rangers Supporters Winter Dress: blue polyester Rangers shirt, faded jeans and *Adidas* sneakers. That was it. Maybe there was something in their *Irn-Bru* which had some magical insulating properties.

I think the entire Constabulary of the Scottish Borders must have been packed into the tiny ground. The official match attendance was 4,476 but I think 6,476 was more accurate. I was tempted to ask the boys in hi-viz yellow if they had each paid £15, but didn't want to get into the bad books of another 2,000 humans. The other strange thing was that everyone in the police contingent was standing up, looking at everyone in the away supporters end: a bit like chimpanzees staring back with wonderment at humans in a zoo. Maybe the police were admiring the sartorial elegance of the Gers supporters or were drawn to their siren-like chanting, which had commenced just before the game kicked off.

I did suggest to one Police Sergeant that it might be much better for all concerned if they were to all turn around and face the pitch, otherwise they would miss the game, which would be a shame and a complete waste of their hard-earned overtime bonuses - in an era of huge cuts to the Police Forces budgets. I wondered whether he was the son of the octogenarian Boadicea in *Asda* - as the pit bull's response was to stick his face into mine and snarl: 'One more smart**** comment like that from you sonny boy and I'll have you cuffed, escorted out of the ground and thrown into the cells.'

## What is wrong with these people???

I resisted the temptation to ask him how long he had been serving in the Scottish Borders Constabulary **Community Relations** Team.

If I had been a Viking 1,200 years ago, I think I would have raided somewhere else where the local population were a bit more cordial and the weather a bit less cold. Maybe La Rochelle or Benidorm.

I was then given a Dogger Bank Warning by the blackcurrant fruit pastille gorging tyrant: 'Just remember. Keep your mouth shut and don't mention anything about Celtic, your favourite colour being green, me deserving to be damned for missing church on Sundays or the Pope… and, for the love of God, don't make any Protestant wisecracks.'

I quietly nodded with silent acquiescence, mainly on account of spotting the Venus of Berwick: a scrumptious blonde lady PC. I wasn't the only one to spot her and it wasn't long before all the 3,000 Gers fans were serenading her with a quaint little song - most likely a traditional Gaelic love song (though I couldn't recall it being played at Celtic Connections). It went along the lines of:

*'Get your* (something unintelligible)'

> *'Get your* (something unintelligible)'
> *'Get your* (something unintelligible) *out for the lads…'*
> *Get your*
> (something <u>unintellllllllllligible</u>)
> *out for the lads…'*

I think Pinkerton may have wooed his Japanese girlfriend with a similar ditty in Act I Scene 2 but, as it was sung in Italian, I could not be sure.

She just put her pretty head down and smiled bashfully. It must have been nice to have so many compliments and admirers at one time.

Having warmed up their larynxes, the Gers started singing some of their other favourite tunes. Something about we are the people and living under a Union Flag. They even started singing God Save the Queen, which I thought was a nice touch. I didn't have her down as a football fan, but I expect she has *Sky TV* at home, so could have been watching it live.

Due to their heavy Glaswegian dialects, I couldn't understand much of what the Gers fans were singing, but the Police were so impressed that they started filming them. Perhaps this was so they could show the rest of the lads back at the police station who had missed out on tickets for the game.

After 10 minutes of being recorded - for what I presumed to be the 'Songs of the Scottish Borders Constabulary Choir and Esteemed Friends 2013' - the Rangers fans felt suitably honoured to start singing:

*'Yer ken stick yer* (something unintelligible) *camera up your a\*\*\*'*
*'Yer ken stick yer* (something unintelligible) *camera up your a\*\*\*'*
*'Yer ken stick yer* (something unintelligible) *camera'*
*'Stick yer* (something unintelligible) *camera'*
*'Stick yer* (something unintelligible) *camera up your a\*\*\*'*

It seemed quite a nice little ditty, maybe it was a traditional 16th century weaver's song from Jura, as I couldn't recall it being amongst Pavarotti's Greatest Hits.

After six minutes, Berwick somehow managed to take the lead, though I thought it would have been fairer had the goal been awarded to Rangers - as it was a Rangers defender who glanced it into the net, past his own keeper, with the most skilful of touches. Being a quasi-supporter of Berwick Rangers for the afternoon, I couldn't resist jumping up and punching the air with my front paws in delight.

My moment of joyous cheering came to an abrupt halt, when I received my second wee throttling within as many hours. The supposedly animal-loving Adolf Hitler grabbed me by the throat, lifted me off the ground and stuck his vein-throbbing face - now the colour of a Heart of Midlothian jersey - into mine, whispering with unbridled ire, as though he was an enraged Trappist Abbot:

'What did I tell you about keeping quiet and maintaining a low profile, you idiot? Do you want to get the three of us lynched?'

'You mean… get the *two of us* lynched…' opined Mackem, before drowning out even the drummer with his bellowed proclamation: '…because I'm a staunch Rangers supporter and always will be, until the day I die.'

'Well, at least if you die, you can be reincarnated as a Town Crier,' I gasped contemptuously, with my eyes rolling upwards (though that was due entirely to oxygen deprivation). I did acknowledge though that being six feet off the ground did give me a better view of the match.

There was a faint ripple of applause and cheering from the Home Supporters. The much louder, *foul-mouthed* shouts of abuse from the Away Supporters berated the defender for his incompetence - but I thought it was the deftest of touches that managed to outfox his goalkeeper.

One particular Gers fan - who was standing behind me - was hopping up and down with anger, looking like his diet for the past 23 years had been deep-fried *Mars Bars*, chips and 80/- Beer. He started bellowing:

'Yer nae fit tae whae the shurrt, ye're naaee fiiiit tae whae the shutt.'

*Why do they have to shout everything twice*? I wondered. *Is everyone from Glasgow hard of hearing*?

Mass deafness would explain why they did not move an inch when the announcer on the tannoy asked them several times to move - so they could fit more of their pals into the packed stadium.

Looking at the hapless defender, I thought that his shirt actually fitted him quite nicely, especially compared to the 21 stone, 5 feet 5 inches epitome of sartorial elegance standing just behind me; whose Rangers shirt seemed to stop about 6 inches short of his waistline.

'You're a fine one to talk Humpty McDumpty, you might want to keep hopping up and down for the next 15 minutes as you might burn off some calories,' which I considered harsh, but sound advice.

It became immediately apparent, however, that he had never invested in any personal training sessions as he looked around at his own eye level to see who *he felt* had just insulted him…

'HAE *******SAED THAT? SEY EET TAE MAA FAES AN I'LL ******* NUTT YAE.'

At which point, Humpty became the new object of attention for the Police's 'Our Day Out At Friendly Berwick' DVD. But the *Weight Watchers* delinquent failed to spot me as I was totally concealed by his 44 inch, *Mars Bar* munching, chip chomping, beer guzzling, Diabetes Type 2-welcoming gut.

He continued his foul-mouthed rant so, tiring of the obese fool, I turned my attention back to the game and spotted Skip and Mackem kneeling on the floor with their hands clasped together looking skywards...

*They must be praying for a Rangers equaliser, which just goes to show that, to some people, football really is more important than life or death*, though Skip was mumbling something concerning me and a bolt of lightning (must have been the beer from the previous evening).

The (Protestant) God must have been watching on EPSN as their prayers did not go unheeded. Three minutes after Rangers had taken the lead, Rangers equalised from a penalty: *This must be what it is like watching chameleons play football,* I mused. *I wouldn't want to be the Ref for all the Cat Master Chef food in Asda.*

The whole ground erupted with such force it was as though an asteroid had hit the ground (the next best thing to a lightning bolt). White and blue streamers were suddenly hurled towards the pitch, narrowly missing a very stern-looking Police Inspector. I had a sneaking suspicion that they were being deliberately aimed at her. From this moment, the Rangers Fans did not stop singing and 3,000 of the 3,003 residents in the Away End kept jumping up and down singing 'Bouncy Bouncy'. They even brought their own drummer to dictate the tempo, until he lost his drumstick but, being the fine upstanding lady she is, PC Venus kindly picked it up and gave it back to him.

Suitably inspired, I impetuously took off my flea collar swung it around my head - like a feline David with his sling - (though with less violent intentions) then cast it towards her.

I was not quite sure where it landed, but Sergeant Pit Bull snarled to his yellow coated terriers as it glided serenely in her general direction: **'WHO THREW THAT BLOODY MISSILE???'**

'Sarge, it was that fat kid, who's been using foul language and threatening to head butt everyone. The one stood next to that blue moggy which looks like it's been half-strangled.'

'Well spotted, Campbell, we'll cuff him at half time and charge him with both a public order offence and threatening behaviour. Keep a close eye on him.'

'Sergeant Pit Bull, how about Campbell and I go in and arrest him now? We could charge him for dropping five *Bounty Bar* wrappers and sneaking in a cat without buying a ticket for it. That scraggy-looking moggy is a major health hazard sat near the burger bar. It'll give everyone E.coli. We could arrest both of them and…'

'Constable Ireton, how many times do I have to tell you? PUT YOUR TRUST IN CCTV AND KEEP YOUR POWDER DRY.'

'Och Sarge, go easy on the poor laddie. Ireton's just come back from a 2 week Kick Boxing Camp in Laavuloooongthaam Laydeebooy in Bangkok. He's nae bin the same since, must've bin the food, and he's still a wee bit jumpy. I could go in ann arrest him on maa own as I've brought a spare truncheon ann maa brand new Nunchaku. Ann I've also brought along *Glencoe* and *Edward Longshanks,* maa wee Neapolitan Mastiffs. They're presently guarding the Police Dog Transport Van and drooling for a wee bit o' action,' piped the ever-willing PC Campbell.

'Just stay where you are Campbell. May I remind you that we are NOT here to extirpate the Rangers Clan. And tell Ireton to wipe off that mascara. He looks like a Panda…'

'….FOR GOD'S SAKE IRETON, STOP PLUCKING YOUR EYEBROWS AND GIVE VENUS BACK HER MIRROR. YOU'RE SUPPOSED TO BE KEEPING YOUR EYES ON THE CROWD,' barked a decreasingly phlegmatic Sergeant Pit Bull.

'Sorry Sarge, it's just that if I am going to be on TV then I want to look my best. I'm hoping the game will be shown live on Channel USO-Hoornie in Thailand,' explained PC Ireton meekly.

Rangers duly took the lead on the stroke of half time: 3,001 residents in the Away End went mad with unbridled joy, whilst one went berserk with unbridled rage - screaming abuse at his *smartphone*… whilst belting it with his remaining *Bounty Bar*. The other less-noisy resident admitted he missed the goal - having become besotted with the beautiful blonde PC Venus.

'If only yon fair lady was a Chartreuse', I lamented.

As the half-time whistle blew, Captain *'I'm buying a ****** Apple i-phone next time'* Bligh and the more serene Coxswain Mackem, who kindly offered to bring me back some milk in a polystyrene cup, went to get some *Bovril*. Not a bad lad really, though he once threatened to kill me when I told him I thought he was from Newcastle - as people from Newcastle and Sunderland all sound the same to me. Fundamentally, I cannot understand any of them. I think: *'Why ay, man, shezza cannae lass'*, was intended to be a compliment for PC Venus.

Anyway, I was standing on the balcony at the front, minding my own business – watching the delectable, bonnie, blonde, PC Venus when a huge Police Inspector came charging towards me, accompanied by two Constables who were so immense they must have been on anabolic steroids.

**'That's one of them. Cuff him, Campbell.'**

'Aye Sir. Can I try out maa new truncheon on him please?' Campbell asked with unbridled zeal, as though he was a Trooper in the 11$^{th}$ Dragoons imploring the Duke of Cumberland to grant him permission to test his new sabre.

'Calm down, Campbell, there is no need to butcher him.'

Then they charged towards me.

**Why me??? What have I done?**

Due to the extreme stress, my fur went spiky, as though I had been electrocuted and my eyes took on the appearance of giant milk saucers (for the first time since I thought I was going to die during the previous December). I stood there petrified, thinking this is totally unjustified harassment.

What were they going to arrest me for? Loitering with intent to applaud the next Rangers goal or for staring longingly at PC Venus?

I admit that I was admiring her, desperately wishing she could be instantly reincarnated as a Chartreux or Burmese, but that hardly amounted to stalking, and I had been too polite to ask her to get her *whatever they were* out for the lads. Then a dreadful thought occurred to me. Perhaps it was the erstwhile Lt. Pinkerton in his post-operatic career - as a member of the Scottish Borders Constabulary - seeking revenge on me, for supposedly doing to his career what he had done to Coco Pop.

Just as I contemplated making a mad dash for it across the giant circular litter tray, they veered to my right and grabbed hold of the portly young Gers behind me, who resembled the *Michelin Man* after overindulging at a tattoo convention.

He was 'cuffed' i.e. had his hands tied together in a weird looking metal device which wouldn't look out of place in a Vet's surgery... perhaps the Berwick fans had complained about his clapping?

He was led off, being told he would be spending the rest of the weekend in custody at Berwick Police Station. Then about six of his mates surrounded me and started enquiring of the Police rather belligerently: 'Wha's he bin lifted?' which I thought was fair enough, as he looked too fat to be picked up.

'For a public order offence, specifically sectarian chanting, and threatening behaviour…' was the curt response.

It carried the intonation that this group of six human - and damned by association, one feline - inquisitors would share the same fate if they continued with their aggressive line of questioning.

Must admit, I didn't recall any chanting besmirching any secretaries - unless it was aimed at Neil Lennon's Personal Assistant.

The debate then dragged on about when he would be granted bail, with the increasingly agitated constable being joined by about 20 other constables. This Scottish/Mexican standoff lasted for what seemed like an eternity - before the Protestant Inquisitors rejoined the rest of the Rangers fans.

Just when I thought this weekend could not possibly get any worse, one of them turned around and marched back to me (*uh, oh, the Catholic cat's out of the bag… now I'm really in trouble*). He picked me up and held me aloft, like a furry trophy… shouting to the other 2,999 Gers Fans:

'Look what I just found lads. A blue cat. He must be one o' us. Let's adopt him as our wee mascot.'

This led to a huge cheer and much drumming, as though I had scored a last-minute winner for Rangers at Ibrox. Then my new found companion asked the others what name they should give me.

As I was about to say I was quite content with Nelson, someone had an orange-hued brainwave and shouted '**Let's call him King Billy!!**' which was met with a huge, approving chorus of cheering by my new papist-hating chums.

**'Hey, King Billy, give a wave of your wee paw to Coisty.'**

Now, I am sure that it looked on live Scottish TV as though I was indeed waving my paw at Coisty, but I would just like to say to any of my Celtic pals who were watching the match at the time, or are reading this now, that it was totally involuntary on my part - due to the maniac shaking my front right leg (like one of those Japanese good fortune-beckoning cats one sees in Teppanyaki Restaurants). To make matters even worse, they all shouted in unison:

> 'Coisty, Coisty, give us a wave.
> Coisty, give us a wave.'

He duly obliged... and topped my increasingly catastrophic day.

My nightmare reached its zenith when they adapted one of their favourite chants in my honour:

'We are the people and we live under the Union Flag. King Billy's our loyal wee mascot and wee pet cat who will forever smite the evil Fenian, Papist Rat.'

I didn't recall this being in *The Magic Flute* during the serene soirée at Nene's house on Bonfire Night, so was going to ask what on earth they were singing about - before remembering that I was in the doghouse with 2,002 humans already. But I did feel like interjecting with my overwhelming desire to be excused so I could go home and practise my own dribbling skills with my multi-coloured ping-pong balls.

In a state of double euphoria at having scored a third goal and having acquired a new mascot, they started to jump up and down again singing: 'Bouncy Bouncy' whilst continually throwing their new mascot up and down in the air. This was the closest I've ever been to doing an Axl Rose body surfing impersonation although by this point I had decided that Berwick-upon-Tweed was not my idea of a paradisal city.

They stopped momentarily, when they spotted a ginger-haired ball boy who probably wished he had kept his job at *Friedbullsass del Rey* when they started chanting:

'Are you Lennon in disguise? Are you Leennnonnn in disguise??? '

They finally put me down with 5 minutes to go but I had performed so many somersaults that an off duty waiter from the 'Celestial Scallop Cantonese Seafood Restaurant' in downtown Berwick, wanted to sign me up for the South Shields Zen Temple Funky Monks Acrobatics Troupe.

As my head was spinning and my eyes were going round like Catherine's Wheels, I did not notice that someone had draped a blue, white and red scarf around my neck.

They then held their shoes in the air and started a new chant, which didn't involve their mascot, thank the Lord (of either denomination, as by this time, I didn't care).

It looked like an advert for *Adidas* sneakers. Having been asked to high-five every one of the 3,000 members in the Away Supporters end, less the two who had been arrested for public disorder offences, I staggered back to my original vantage point, musing… *maybe I should have taken my chances with Pinkerton after all*.

**I had never been so delighted to see El Capitan.**

But I got the slightest of impressions that this sentiment was not entirely reciprocated…

'You blithering bloody idiot. You stupid, in-bred, braindead ******* cat…

(I found this foul-mouthed and scurrilous piece of bile to be particularly offensive. If he had added Catholic, Papist or fenian as an extra adjective, I could have reported him for secretarial abuse).

'Who did you steal that Rangers scarf from? You mindless, feline moron? Do you want us all to get hauled off into the middle of that baying mob and beaten up for stealing? Did you not see what they've been doing to that rag doll for the last half hour? Imagine what it would be like if they were throwing you up in the air like that, non-stop for 30 minutes…'

*I may be a mindless moron, but at least I'm not a myopic moron…* I thought to myself.

I had a good mind to turn back to my new found Loyalist mates, who were proving to be most pleasant, and tell them that they did indeed have a Fenian, Papist rat of the human variety in their midst. And that he was of the foul-mouthed, cat abusing, sub-variety.

But I just lay down, mentally shattered, ruminating: 'O death, where is thy sting?' which in the circumstances was quite apt (1 Corinthians 15:55-56 King James' Version).

His Mackem Lieutenant commented on how funny it was to see me in a Rangers scarf and he suggested taking a photo which he could load onto *Facebook,* then all of his mates in Lanarkshire could see it.

Well, why not? Could this day possibly get any worse…?

This had become one of those days where I wished I had just never risen off my bean bag. But despite feeling exhausted, I felt compelled to stand up for myself and tell them of my own secretarial predicament. So… I turned round to the Rangers fans, who were by now all waving enthusiastically at me, giving me the thumbs up, telling me that I was a *'spunky wee laddie'* and they were honoured to call me one of their own. Some were even taking pictures of me on their mobile phones and, I have to say, generally being very amiable. I thought: *They're not such a bad bunch after all.*

They had even given me an empty bottle of *Irn-Bru*, which they had filled with 36 small capsules of long-life milk purloined from the chippie behind the stand.

I was about to explain that:

'My real name is Nelson. I am deeply flattered that you have chosen to call me King Billy but, if I am to be given a sobriquet I would rather it be Saint Patrick or Jock Stein.'

With a look of terror on his face - as though he was a Christian about to be thrown to my larger ancestors - Mein Führer shoved a huge catnip snake into my mouth (ironically green with a gold tongue) in order to shut me up - but did so with such enormous force that he sent me flying backwards.

It was as though I had been fired in reverse out of a fairground cannon. I only halted when the rear of my cranium connected at speed with a concrete slab - duly knocking me out.

Just as I was falling into unconsciousness, I could see the feline thumper being surrounded by about 400 enraged Gers supporters and only the rapid intervention of as many Policemen prevented him from being lynched.

The next thing I knew, I was lying down - the headache at the front of my cranium now being accompanied by one at the rear - in a *St. John's*

*Ambulance* under a Royal Stewart blanket and with an oxygen mask over my face.

As I blearily opened my eyes, I thought I must be hallucinating, as there sitting next to me was an angel... PC Venus-Flora MacDonald. She was holding my front right paw and checking my pulse (which was infinitely more agreeable - with respect - than having it be used to wave at Coisty). Plus... she was weeping gently: 'I thought we'd lost him...'

*Maybe Berwick isn't so bad after all*, I mused, as I felt a sudden and overpowering Winston-inspired urge to spring into charm mode. Just when I thought this evening couldn't possibly get any better she said, in a lovely, soft, lilting, hybrid, Anglo-Scottish-Asda accent:

'He looks so cute wrapped in that wee tartan rug. I could take the wee laddie home with me and give him a good cuddle.'

After all the physical, emotional and verbal abuse of several hours earlier, I was suddenly starting to feel like the cat's whiskers. I could not have been happier had I been floating in an urn of Jersey Milk. I felt my round copper eyes evolving into red hearts and only my desire to milk this moment for all it was worth prevented me from leaping onto her shoulder - akin to the Argentinean winger: Luiz Megadolla- Onbirdsanbooz, recovering from two broken legs to convert a $90^{th}$ minute winning penalty against England.

I henceforth decided that my Rod Stewart cat collar was actually quite debonair.

I spent the night as the guest of honour at Berwick Police Station, where even the previously cat-cursing Inspector Pinkerton was nice to me.

At 19:00 hrs I was given fresh milk, rolled oats and venison and spent most of the night ensuring that I was sitting on the lap of PC Venus-Flora MacDonald. I was purring so loudly that I could have been used as a police siren for the whole of the Scottish Borders. The only sad note was that, despite my best efforts to impersonate an Alsatian, my application to enlist as a sniffer dog was rejected.

I almost forgot to mention what happened to my LHC. As a result of his act of gratuitous violence, the cat clobberer was arrested for GBH and spent the night in the cells getting acquainted with 11 drunken Rangers fans, who at first, irately refused to believe he was the: '…caring, proud and devoted owner of their team mascot'.

I only found this out while being given a post-dinner tour of the station at 21:00 hrs. I spotted the heinous, animal abusing criminal in Cell 5 with his newly-acquainted Rangers mates.

**He had never been so delighted to see me.**

However, I gave him the indubitable impression that this sentiment was not at all reciprocated. The grovelling sycophant greeted me thus:

'Nelson, you cannot imagine how overjoyed I am to see you, my *devoted little companion*! (*non-insured,* I was tempted to interject, presuming the Scarborough Warning had sailed off - along with his dignity). Please help me get out of here as soon as possible. These guys are lunatics. If they find out I'm Catholic they'll string me up.'

The '…blithering bloody idiot' of four hours earlier considered this hyperbolic & pusillanimous - albeit genuine plea for assistance - for a minute, before giving him my quixotic response:
'I do not mix with criminals… and I am certainly not accustomed to helping them escape from jail.'

I then cocked my only slightly throbbing head to one side and jauntily sauntered off to inspect the Glaswegian inmates of Cells 6 to 20 (except Cell 19 which held an inebriated local, dressed as a rooster) - already feeling distaste at having to come into contact with such riff-raff.

As I bid a fond Bonne Nuit à Jean Valjean, I could hear his acquaintances telling him to relax as they were often arrested on match days -  meaning they rarely had to pay for overnight accommodation or breakfast - for a wide range of offences such as urinating in public, being drunk and disorderly or for threatening behaviour. They said that the maximum custodial sentence they had ever received was a paltry nine weeks.

Clearly not being 100% comfortable with the prospect of a nine-week vacation, courtesy of HMP Alcatrazington, they reassured him that, as this was his first offence, he would get off with just a caution. They also stated that when they were bailed on the Monday morning, they would club together and treat him to a free 'Rangers Forever' tattoo all the way across his back.  I was busy inspecting the recalcitrant inmates of Cell 7 when I heard PC

Venus-Flora MacDonald launch a vitriolic attack on one unfortunate inmate in Cell 5:

'**PEOPLE LIKE YOU DISGUST ME,** hitting a poor defenceless little animal like that. What did that innocent little cat ever do to you, 'ey, big man??? Give you some cheek? Make some smart**** comment at your expense? Display an act of brazen impudence? Did he show you a total lack of respect... in your warped, evil, twisted mind?'

Before he had the opportunity to answer in the affirmative to all, or even just one of the above, she smote him down with a succinct, but acerbic tongue lashing - sharper than a highlander's broadsword.

'And I've heard you've got previous. Lucky for you it happened overseas, so it would be inadmissible in court here. But if it was up to me, I'd have you hung, drawn and quartered.'

At this point, a Police Sergeant told her she was going over the top somewhat and to calm down as:

'Ken yer nae see ye're alarming the wee blue moggie? Ah think he's suffered enough fir one day.'

I begged to differ, thinking: *'Seems fair enough to me,'* as I ran around in circles punching the air with glee.

PC Flora had revealed a hitherto hidden, steely side to her otherwise angelic personality - but I realised this had to be a prerequisite for policing in these wild and lawless parts of the British Isles.

Sir Joshua Reynolds could not have painted a better portrait of the aghast expression on the visage of the cat clobberer... who could not have looked more distraught had someone informed him that he had won £25 million on the *National Lottery* 2 minutes after putting his winning ticket though a paper shredder.

At the end of this figurative broadside - which would have impressed Captain Bligh - the villain's roommates stood motionless, having meekly lost the urge to beseech Flora to get her (*something unintelligible*) out for the lads. They were quieter than a group of Trappist Monks - which was appropriate, bearing in mind the vast quantities of *Leffe Blonde & Bruin* they had consumed before being arrested.

I did think the look of sheer dread on their faces suggested that they had been told the Spanish Inquisition would be down in 10 minutes to convert them to Catholicism - once they had finished assembling their rack and drunk their café con leches.

Flora then caught my longing eye and her gaze immediately mellowed saying:

'Dinnae worry boot him, sweetheart. When we go back oopstairs I'll give ye a wee card with maa mobile number on it an' yer ken call me straightaway if he even *threatens* to touch you again.'

*'Hmm, sounds good to me. Does that include worming?'* I purred to myself, with unequivocal glee.

The twelve miscreants incarcerated in Cell 5 were all straining their necks to see who exactly she was talking to - being slightly concerned that the pressure of policing, exacerbated by the looming threat of police cuts, of a magnitude only a criminal mastermind could have imposed on them, was affecting her.

But their puzzled and, I have to say, jealous stares (barring that of one particularly vicious brute) were set 5 feet too high to see the object of her fully reciprocated affection.

I sat there grinning like a Cheshire Cat, thinking - after everything I had been through - I was enjoying this soliloquy, and almost everything Berwick had to offer.

The next morning, I was asked, with much anticipation, if I wanted to press charges against the vicious brute. I was sorely tempted, but said that I would like to think about it over a delightful breakfast of kippers.

Though sorely tempted, thinking about all the threats, the insults, the gratuitous cuff across the brow, and last, but not least, the smack in the mouth with a catnip snake covered fist... I decided, in a further quixotic display of nobility, inherent in British Shorthairs - to decline.

But, there was one condition:
'I wish to feed the cat-hating criminal a *McVitie's* biscuit for breakfast.'

They put my - what seemed to them - most bizarre request down to concussion, with the added bonus that I was able to lie on Flora's lap for roughly another 48 minutes 23 blissful seconds, whilst she tapped away at a computer. I think she was writing something to the RSPCA - asking their Leeds branch to be vigilant regarding a cat-abusing hoodlum. Then she browsed the website of the Contented Cat Magazine, to see where she could get hold of a 10-week old version of myself.

I thought *'Why waste valuable police time (and overtime) surfing the Internet when you could have me?'* feeling strangely like Coco Pop's unwanted young son. But, at least, she didn't try to commit hara-kiri with her truncheon.

At 10.00 a.m. on the Sunday morning, the feline thumper was released from custody and his less than impressed Mackem mate - plus mugged moggie victim - were waiting to accompany him back to Sunderland.

Flora came over to wish me a fond farewell and reminded me about her mobile number. Jack the Mackem lad's ears pricked up at this point and he resembled Doctor Spock.

'You're such a lovely wee laddie, you're welcome to come and visit me any time (*that's me... not Jack the Mackem Lad*). I just know Sooty maa pet Beagle would get on with yer like a huus on fire.'

**'Sooty ... the Beagle ???'**

My hopes were deflated more quickly than Cadel Evans' tyres when a French vélo-terrorist spread tacks across the road in last year's Tour de France.

Meanwhile, the Mackem Lothario was 'in like Flynn' and spent the next 75 minutes asking if he could have the pleasure of introducing himself to:

'…truly the most bonnie police lady he had ever cast his world-weary eyes on', and generally being a sycophantic nuisance.

I tried telling the Bard of Wearside that Burns Night had been celebrated 3 weeks earlier, but he only halted his soliloquy when Flora threatened him with incarceration in the presently vacant Cell 5. So… he took his leave with a Robbie Burns inspired piece of plagiarism which fooled no-one:

> Ae fond kiss, and then we sever;
> Ae fareweel, and then forever!'
> Fare thee weel, thou first and fairest!
> Fare thee weel, thou best and dearest!

*What is he going on about?? Is he still drunk? Perhaps it's the sea air or indulging in one too many Belhavens the previous evening…* I thought to myself.

Looking at the bemused expression on Flora's face, I think she thought exactly the same.

On the way home, the Bard kept waxing lyrical about bonnie lassies in the Scottish Borders Constabulary, whilst I peered out of the front windscreen (having a front passenger seat on the journey back was 17$^{th}$ on my list of conditions for not pressing charges) - but then, I thought, I have Kiku waiting for me when I get back home. And the Yorkshire Yakuza has Nene loyally waiting for him - like the heroine of Madame Butterfly.

I looked back at the ex-con with a cocked eyebrow - the one that was not assaulted - thinking that I know what he is thinking… *and he knows what I am thinking* viz. Nene will be highly unimpressed to find out that her new Beau now actually has a pan-

European criminal record. This is after telling her parents that he is a charming, lovely guy with impeccable manners.

'Personality traits common to all psychopaths,' I assured myself, feeling quite relaxed that the psychopath in residence would be forever in my favour from this day on.

I promised Jacques Mesrine that I would not tell her about his dark, violent side.

With a look of utter distrust in his eyes he confided in _me_ (in which case he must really be worried...):

'The more I protest my innocence, the more I will be condemned as guilty in her eyes.'

Which I thought sounded classically romantic, as though he was Aeneas (another philandering bounder who, ipso facto, must be an ancestor of Winston) lamenting about Dido.

I finally deigned to agree... on a couple of reasonable conditions, which I insisted be witnessed by a lawyer:

1. I am NEVER to be neutered, nor threatened with such surgical procedure.
2. Dry cat food will be forever consigned to history (and so will Sterilised French Milk).
3. I am to be served only: *Cat Master Chef* Cordon Bleu Cuisine.
4. Kiku can move in... and she gets her own bean bag and litter tray - with a curtain on top.
5. He sends a Christmas Card every year to PC Venus-Flora MacDonald, on my behalf.

6.     He buys 4 tickets for 8 Berwick Rangers home games for the next 12 seasons.

7.     I get a daily allowance of 4 large saucers of Jersey Milk… until further notice. Including, when overseas, on holiday. Even if we fly to the moon.

8.     He renews my pan-European Pet Insurance Cover - in perpetuity (not to be construed as only valid within the city walls of Perpignan). This has to cover both myself and Kiku.

9.     He is to clean out my litter tray every day - and use organic cat litter only… and never wrap tinsel around my litter tray ever again.

10.    He is never to accuse me of being impudent, disrespectful, opportunistic, ungrateful, a mindless moron, a smart****, unreasonable or a Machiavellian little git… ever again.

# March

As my diary draws to a close, Rick-san and Nene-san, Kiku-san and *moi* visit *Kendell's Bistro* in what should be classed as Leeds' French Quarter for yet another divine evening of superlative Gallic cuisine, making me realise how much better British food would have been had Napoléon won at Waterloo.

**The Last Plantagenet King**

I have just learned that the bones of the much-maligned King Richard III have been found under a supermarket car park in Leicester.

*Must have been where he made his last stand…* I thought, trying to picture him fighting off the Lancastrian hordes and those of the treacherous Sir William Stanley - amongst the Fruit & Veg section.

I didn't realise that supermarkets in the late 15th century sold horses - so they haven't really come on much in 500 years.

And I really don't know what all the fuss is about regarding horsemeat. The French eat horses all the time.

I do believe that it would be a huge injustice to bury Richard III in Leicester Cathedral. Despite being the Duke of Gloucester, he should be buried in York Minster - as he was the last Yorkist King and he served as Lord President of the Council of the North from 1472 to 1483… and he was immensely popular with the good, loyal folk of Yorkshire.

To build on a quote from Hamlet:

'The cat will mew, the dog will have his day, Richard III will have his burial in York.'

I think it was largely due to the Bard of Tudor Propaganda that Richard III has been such an unfairly maligned monarch. During his brief reign, he had been fondly referred to as *'Good King Richard'*. He ameliorated the criminal legal system, such as introducing bail and the 15$^{th}$ century equivalent of legal aid, and generally tried to improve the welfare of the common people, unlike the Machiavellian breed of Tudor miscreants who usurped him. Despite Richard III's coat of arms being a White Boar, I would say it should have been a British Shorthair, bearing in mind how much my ancestors were persecuted (due to bigotry and ignorance) during the Middle Ages. Then, once all the cats had been murdered, the rat population flourished and that led to the Black Death in the 14$^{th}$ century - which killed a third of the population - and the Great Plague of London in the 1660s.

*Humans really do seem to have an irrational proclivity for self-destruction,* I reflected, sadly. Yet another reason why I think humans are buffoons.

Shakespeare also assassinated the character of Macbeth - King of Scotland - and fanned the flames of anti-Semitic bigotry with the Merchant of Venice. That's why I have always preferred Dickens.

I have not met any Jewish cats, but I am sure they are very nice and no different from any other breed - apart from declining *Cat Master Chef* Pork Cutlets.

Which begs the question... why can't humans just accept and tolerate each other's differences, whether political, religious or breed - all of which would make the world a much happier place.

'Surely everyone throughout the world can learn to co-exist harmoniously?' The Emcee from-the Kit Kat Klub in Berlin pondered, and that was back in 1931, so humans have made lamentably little progress during the last 80 years – and that's despite *Facebook*...

Having said that, I cannot say I am particularly enamoured of Beagles, Jehovah's Witnesses or Pinkerton.

This has been quite an eventful period in my life and things are looking up for both myself and Rick-san. He is trying to master Japanese Cooking and the saxophone - whilst I am hoping to master the art of Haiku, which is more difficult than expected. Apparently, creating each haiku poem involves 3 portions of 5 then 7 then another 5 syllabubs... so I am worried that I may have ballooned in weight by the time I write my next book, which, having been inspired by Sun Tzu and Miyamoto Musashi (Kiku pleaded that I read the latter on pain of death by 1,000 roundhouse kicks), is to be entitled: 'Nelson and the Art of War.'

## Nelson's Haiku Verses

C'est Le Tour de France
Only mad dogs and rosbifs
Cycle in heatwave

It's August in France
Les Chasseurs are on the hunt
Absinthe, guns, not good mix

Just before midnight
The world is about to end
Claws clipped, defenceless

Winter in Berwick
Involuntary mascot
I'm a Cat'olic

Kiku very cute cat
Serene as cherry blossom
When not strangling me

Having grown weary of the drudgery of the corporate world, with its guaranteed salary each month and sick pay, holiday pay, subsidised restaurant, unwritten compulsion to devote many long, hard hours to buffooning about on *Facebook*, annual bonuses, enduring many more hours picking fantasy football teams each week and the pension scheme etc. Rick-san is hoping to get his own business off the ground.

**Junk Mail and Boadicea Ding Dong Communications**

My LHC continues to be bombarded by letters from a debt collection agency, acting on behalf of *Boadicea Ding Dong Communications*. Despite his numerous attempts to tell them that their non-paying customer has never lived at our home, and neither of us have ever heard of him, they continue to send increasingly threatening letters, demanding immediate payment. I can sense that he is beside himself with stress, so I put a friendly paw on his shoulder and told him not to worry as: '…your much maligned feline companion, Nelson, has loped along to the rescue'.

This is my response…

To:
**My favourite bloodhounds at BIFFO Debt Busters**

Subject:
**The elusive, non-paying, Mr. Percy Blake-Dunnarunna**

I did try phoning you again this evening, but assume you could not (ironically) find the phone - as it rang out for over 20 minutes before I accepted defeat.

This is just a short note of appreciation for your latest letter, dated 6th March 2013, which was addressed to the phantom Mr. Percy Blake-Dunnarunna who, for reasons known exclusively to yourselves and *Boadicea Ding Dong Communications* , you insist resides at my home: 1805 Trafalgar Boulevard, Moggieforth, West Yorkshire.

I have to say that I admire your dogged persistence in pursuing said scoundrel, who has a share-value-shattering unpaid bill of £54.96.

I recall my earlier phone calls to the *Boadicea Ding Dong Communications* Debt Collections Team - and your good selves - explaining vainly that he does not reside at this address, and never has done in the 9 years 11 months that I have lived here.

That is, unless, of course, he is squatting in my cellar. In which case, I shall set a trap this evening and leave lots of un-ironed washing out. If I find any of it has been ironed, even just one humble sock, then this will endorse your intuition and I shall apologise profusely.

Or… he could be hiding in the attic… perhaps you could send some former members of the Gestapo round to my house to scour the attic and flush him out, though I realise there may not be many left, as I would estimate the minimum age of any surviving members to be at least 90.

It would be futile sending any ex-Gestapo members if they have zimmer frames or hip replacements, due to the fact they will have to mount three flights of stairs and may risk death or serious injury in their line of duty for BIFFO Debt Busters, for which, no doubt, I will be sued for the minimum sum of £55.96 for gross negligence.

You have kindly informed me in your letter of 6th March 2013 that your field agents will: 'VISIT YOUR ADDRESS TO COLLECT THE OUTSTANDING BALANCE'.

I dare not presume whether this friendly notification is addressed to the clearly shy & retiring Percy or to myself. I have, however, always prided myself on my hospitality to any guests... excluding Mormons or Jehovah's Witnesses - so would be grateful if you could kindly provide some advance notice, as I would need to put the kettle on. Please also let me know whether they would prefer *Lavazza*, *Nescafe Gold Blend, Nescafe Decaf* or - if they are on secondment from the Lima office of BIFFO Debt Busters - *Cap Colombie*.

I also have some Moroccan Mint Teabags if they do not like non-organic or unfair trade coffee - which seems to be 'de rigeur' in these cash-strapped times. When they do arrive, could you please ask them to ring the bell - rather than bash down the front door with a sledgehammer, as I have just finished repainting it in a lovely shade of *De Luxe Napoleonic Blue,* which cost me £56.96.

When I spoke to the (clearly hard of hearing) company Rottweiler at the *Boadicea Ding Dong Communications* Contact Centre, Miss Isla Ripyerspleenoutifyerdoonpay, to explain that (a) Mr. Blake-Dunnarunna does not live here and (b) neither my cat, Nelson, nor I have ever heard of him - she displayed her indisputably admirable skills in customer relations, by suggesting that *I* go round to all of my neighbours, to ask if he is living with any of them. Bearing in mind that none of my parsimonious neighbours even sent me a Xmas Card last December, it may be safe to assume that I am not overly popular with the local residents or their 57,960 *Facebook* Friends… and that is without my implying that they may be harbouring a ding dong fugitive.

Whilst Boadicea Ding Dong Communications expects every man and his cat to do his debt-collecting duty, it is with great sorrow that I have to inform you that Nelson is even less popular with my neighbours than myself; on account of having allegedly butchered Villeneuve and Federico, the pet canaries of Hilary Kingfisher who resides at No 1807, last Christmas. I reminded her that she was forever complaining that they never did sing much, but this did not assuage her grief. I did help Mrs Kingfisher bury the somewhat eviscerated canaries under a delightful rose bush in her front garden, since when Nelson has been using their joint graves as a latrine whenever he decides that his litter tray in our kitchen is too full for his liking.

This is quite a common occurrence and has not so far helped to win back Mrs Kingfisher's affections… for either of us.

But I do think this is an absolutely splendid example of **'*outside the litter tray*'** thinking by *Boadicea Ding Dong Communications* and I will now, for the rest of my debt-free life, regret transferring to *my current provider* instead of *Boadicea Ding Dong Communications*, when my patience was exhausted by the value-add assassins at my previous Ding-a-Ling broadband supplier - for whom the concept of being even remotely polite and helpful to its customers was about as appealing as a box of windproof matches or Zippo Lighter would have been for Joan of Arc.

I have copied in some of my friends/associates/partners in crime who reside in places ranging from the deepest, darkest corners of rural France, to the sprawling metropolis of Shanghai, and from the mean, streets of sun-drenched Sydney to the leafy suburbs of Leeds and Bradford – in the hope that just one of them will have some inkling of this phantom's whereabouts.

If he is of a superstitious or gullible persuasion then I suspect he may be hiding in a cave near Bugarach in France in which case you could sub-contract 58.96 ex-U.S. Navy Seals to flush him out.

If the current US Administration is anything like our own cost-cutting, redundancy-obsessed *'Holy White Flags. Attention all personnel, lie down and roll over, the combined fleets of Iceland and the*

*Faroe Islands are steaming towards the Henley Regatta'* current government (I can just make out the faintest of sounds emanating from Hades viz. the ghosts of Napoléon, Kaiser Wilhelm and Adolf collectively wailing and gnashing their teeth at this tantalising thought) there must be dozens or scores or even hundreds of unemployed ex-U.S. Navy Seals currently seeking meaningful work.

I will even go the extra mile and ask my garden

gnome to keep an eye out and bludgeon this late-paying parasite over the head with his shovel, until he begs for mercy, if he spots the incorrigible rogue Blake-Dunnarunna lurking behind my garden shed.

If you like, I can go two extra miles by asking my friend in China if, once he has finished knocking on the doors of all 24 million residents in Shanghai, he could possibly pop over to North Korea to see if the aforementioned fugitive is seeking sanctuary there.

It would help in this regard if you could give me some vital details concerning this modern day Scarlet Pimpernel - specifically whether his occupation- is either *'Nuclear Physicist'* or *'Rocket Scientist'*. If so, that would lead me to believe he may indeed be holed up in a penthouse apartment in Pyongyang surfing the Internet at this very moment, compliments of Glorious Illustrious Yoo Hoo Boom Boom Fook Yu Online Media.

Yours sincerely,

The ever-vigilant Rick and Nelson.

Ding Dong.

**Rick's business venture:**

Partners, no money, no trust.

Sadly doomed to fail.

Cordialement,

*Nelson.*

# Acknowledgements

Writing this book has been a novel experience and, on behalf of Nelson, who has been busy watching this year's Tour de France, I would like to cordially thank the following:

Meiko Wakabayashi, who acted tirelessly as my loyal Personal Assistant, spending many an hour liaising with the other wonderful humans listed below; superlatives fail me.

Stella Stocker, who gave Nelson the initial push of encouragement that he needed in order to expand his original short tale into a book. Nelson told me that he never thought he would have a '…cat in hell's chance' of narrating 10,000 words, let alone 50,000.

In-Scribe, for their unflagging patience, encouragement, enthusiasm and support. They offer a service par excellence and are an absolute pleasure to work with.

Dasha Luchinskaya, for her superb paintings of Nelson. We are hoping that Dasha will invite us as guests of honour to her much-heralded exhibition.

Tom Kociemski, who can list Computing Genius amongst his array of talents.

Chris Canning, for his handsome portraits of Nelson throughout the book. I have been asked to point out by a certain British Shorthair that these portraits are highly accurate and not flattering in any way.

D.M. Caslaw Esq. - a travel organiser extraordinaire.

Mike Jones, the landlord of 'The Pig's Arms' in Sydney, Australia, for his encouragement and support.

The gastronomic palace that is 'Le Roman des Saveurs' in Montmorillon, for introducing us to the culinary delights of *le fromage de chèvre*.

Life with Nelson has been a stormy voyage of Trials and Tribulations.

His statement is the closest that he has ever come to displaying a whiff of appreciation for anything I have done for him.

On any future trips to France I will, if possible, place Nelson in temporary exile - a cattery in Elba might be pertinent or, better still, on Saint Helena.

*Rick Vaughan.*

**Nelson's verbatim expressions of his gratitude:**

1. Jersey Cows for producing the best milk.

2. The 200,000 Parisians - plus one dog - who attended the Winners' Ceremony of the 2012 Tour de France, '…for not lynching me'.

3. Finally, with clenched paws, and on pain of neutering, I must thank my loyal human companion Rick Vaughan for agreeing to type up my thoughts, musings and recollections. Rick told me through gritted teeth that it was his ineluctable pleasure and not mine. For once, I agree with him.

Thank you / Merci beaucoup/ Doumo arigato gozaimasu.

*Nelson.*

Should you like to follow Nelson, he would cordially invite you to visit his website at:

WWW.NELSONTHECAT.COM

Printed in Great Britain
by Amazon.co.uk, Ltd.,
Marston Gate.